PRESENTED TO

The married Couples I love

BY

Tanaya Moon Morris
to be read and passed around
as needed... .

DATE

December 25, 2013
Merry Christmas

ISBN: 978-1-4336-7959-9
B&H Publishing Group
Nashville, Tennessee
www.BHPublishingGroup.com

Dewey Decimal Classification: 242.64
Love \ Marriage \ Devotional Literature

Printed in the United States of America
1 2 3 4 5 6 7 8 9 10 • 17 16 15 14 13

THE
Love Dare

THE
Love Dare

STEPHEN & ALEX
KENDRICK
WITH LAWRENCE KIMBROUGH

NASHVILLE, TENNESSEE

RECEIVE THIS AS A WARNING.
THIS FORTY-DAY JOURNEY CANNOT
BE TAKEN LIGHTLY.

IT IS A CHALLENGING AND OFTEN
DIFFICULT PROCESS, BUT AN INCREDIBLY
FULFILLING ONE. TO TAKE THIS DARE
REQUIRES A RESOLUTE MIND AND A
STEADFAST DETERMINATION.

IT IS NOT MEANT TO BE SAMPLED OR BRIEFLY
TESTED, AND THOSE WHO QUIT EARLY WILL
FORFEIT THE GREATEST BENEFITS. IF YOU
WILL COMMIT TO A DAY AT A TIME FOR FORTY
DAYS, THE RESULTS COULD CHANGE YOUR
LIFE AND YOUR MARRIAGE.

CONSIDER IT A DARE, FROM OTHERS
WHO HAVE DONE IT BEFORE YOU.

Prepare for the Journey
Author's Preface

When The Love Dare was first published in 2008, no one fully anticipated the response. We were humbled and surprised that it quickly became an international best seller and has remained on The New York Times list for more than three years. Millions of people around the world took the Love Dare journey and began learning and practicing these principles in their relationships. Countless e-mails poured in, sharing how romance was being rekindled, dying marriages were being saved, and eyes were being opened to the nature of true, committed love. Marriage counselors and pastors started using the book to strengthen the couples under their care. Even divorce attorneys and judges were rerouting couples to the movie Fireproof and The Love Dare instead of to court.

We were moved to hear from soldiers returning home from war using The Love Dare to turn around their struggling marriages. Empty nesters shared with delight how they were falling in love again. One man personally went through the book six times with his wife because of how much they were learning and enjoying the experience together. We even heard about an elderly man who stood up at a public event and spontaneously cried out, "I want everyone to know that I just took the Love Dare and have never loved my wife more than I do right now!"

We thank God for every person, marriage, and family that has benefited and been blessed by this journey. We recognize that He is the One who changes hearts and resurrects dead marriages. We are so grateful that He allowed us to join Him in sharing with this generation these timeless truths about love.

So it is with gratefulness that we present this updated

version of *The Love Dare* for your use. It is more than just a new cover. We have carefully gone back through and strengthened almost every chapter from the original manuscript, adding fresh concepts while still maintaining the overall feel and format. We've also provided some new resources in the appendix and shared actual reader responses at the end of each day to encourage you on your journey.

It's still *The Love Dare* . . . only better!

If this is your first time going through, you will discover that some principles may seem simple and second nature to you, while others are new concepts outside of your usual box. The key is not what you already know about love or discover as you read, but what you will actually do and implement into your relationship on a consistent basis. Merely understanding these truths won't transform your marriage. They must be applied to your relationship. Love must be a daily, active verb, not a dormant comprehension or feeling. Anytime you think, "I already know that," you should follow it up with, "But do I *do* that?" We hope this book and experience will jump-start you into a new, dynamic way of thinking and living.

As you begin, here are five questions that have repeatedly surfaced that we would like to answer for you.

1. Should I do the Love Dare alone, or with my spouse?

If your spouse will go through the book with you, then consider reading it together and have fun attempting to "outdo" each other with every dare. If you don't think your spouse will join in, then consider keeping it a secret, and enjoy making them curious, wondering what is going on.

2. What if my spouse finds out and says, "You are only doing all these nice things for me because this book says to do them"?

Simply say something like, "No one is forcing me to do any of these things. I'm choosing to do them. Yes, I'm getting ideas from a book, but the reason I'm reading it in the first place is because I want to become a more loving person and learn to better express love to you. Now that you know about this, I dare you to go through it with me."

3. *What if I fall behind and can't keep up?*

Don't feel guilty if you can't follow every dare perfectly. Go at your own pace. If you struggle at any point, then remember that moving slowly and completing the journey is more important than finishing it in forty days. But do your best and try to keep up, adjusting as needed.

4. *What if I am currently separated or divorced?*

Get creative rather than giving up. Focus on doing what you can feasibly do for your spouse or your ex. Some people in the past have just read the book, saved up dares, and then completed appropriate ones when opportunities arose during limited moments of interaction. Others have turned the dares into prayers for their spouse or completed them through the mail or over the Internet. Simply adapt to your situation and take on the challenge for your own benefit as well. Couples who are separated by job transfers, military duties, or travel schedules can also apply some of these creative approaches and still enjoy the blessings of the experience.

5. *What if my spouse does not respond at all to this?*

Just keep going. This journey is more about you learning to love than how your spouse responds. We've found that some spouses respond well right away. Others just need more time. If there are years of pain and emotional damage built up, it will take greater nourishment and slower healing over time. Even if you do everything right, your spouse may not know how to receive love and may initially react negatively as a test to see how sincere and consistent you are. Be patient and think long-term. One man relentlessly went through *The Love Dare* three times before his wife finally broke and turned back to him to restore their marriage. Even if she had not, what he was learning was priceless to his own life. Never underestimate the power of unconditional love. Take on the challenge and know that you are not alone in this journey, and that others are cheering you on.

We were both reminded recently just how precious the gift of marriage is, when a couple shared with us their personal story of reuniting and being remarried after being divorced for twenty-seven years. We were deeply inspired by their tearful testimony. It confirmed again for us that even during the hardest times, marriage is always priceless and worth fighting for.

Our hope for you is that this adventure will add a fresh dose of the extraordinary to your relationship. Then as you learn new things, be sure to share your story with others to inspire and encourage them in their journey! Dare to love!

Blessings to you,

Stephen and Alex Kendrick
Authors, *The Love Dare*

"*Pursue love.*" (*1 Corinthians 14:1a*)

AND LET US CONSIDER ONE ANOTHER
IN ORDER TO STIR UP LOVE AND GOOD WORKS.

HEBREWS 10:24 NKJV

Where Is Your Marriage Now?
Free Evaluation

In order to help you establish a clear, current snapshot of your marriage and to chart your progress throughout the Love Dare journey, we have developed a FREE, personalized marriage evaluation that's simple, private, online, and anonymous. In just a few minutes, you can quickly clarify where you are, discover your key areas of growth, and identify how to more strategically use *The Love Dare* to benefit you.

Simply go to **www.LoveDareTest.com** and follow the step-by-step instructions. You can take it in fifteen minutes or less, and then watch your analysis and results quickly appear, along with practical recommendations.

Whether you take this evaluation alone or with your spouse, we hope you'll seriously consider starting *The Love Dare* with this helpful information in hand. It will not only give you diagnostic insights about yourself and your marriage, but will also lead you to the specific "days" in the book that are most geared toward strengthening your relationship in several specific areas of marital health. We also encourage you to take the test again after you complete *The Love Dare* so you can compare your results. Enjoy!

NOTE: We are grateful for respected marriage therapist and author Dr. Ramon Presson, who helped us develop this exclusive marriage tool by combining his longtime expertise with the heart of the Love Dare content. Dr. Gary Chapman, author of *The Five Love Languages*, says, "I have personally known Ramon Presson for almost thirty years, and I'm pleased to commend him as a specialist in personal and marriage enrichment. He has the unique ability of unveiling the hurt and pointing the way to hope." We think you'll agree.

Now Let's Begin
Introduction

The Scriptures say that God designed and created marriage as a good thing. It is a beautiful, priceless gift. He uses marriage to help us eliminate loneliness, multiply our effectiveness, establish families, raise children, enjoy life, and bless us with relational intimacy.

But beyond this, marriage also shows us our need to grow and deal with our own issues and self-centeredness through the help of a lifelong partner. If we are teachable, we will learn to do the one thing that is most important in marriage—*to love*. This powerful union provides the path for you to learn how to love another imperfect person unconditionally. It is wonderful. It is difficult. It is life-changing.

This book is about love. It's about learning and daring to live a life filled with loving relationships. And this journey begins with the person who is closest to you: your spouse. May God bless you as you begin this adventure.

But be sure of this: it will take courage. If you accept this dare, you must take the view that instead of *following* your heart, you are choosing to *lead* it. The world tells you to follow your heart, but if you are not leading it, then someone or something else is. The Bible says that "the heart is more deceitful than all else" (Jeremiah 17:9), and it will always pursue that which feels right at the moment.

We dare you to think differently—choosing instead to *lead your heart* toward that which is best in the long run. This is a key to lasting, fulfilling relationships.

The Love Dare journey is not a process of trying to change your spouse to be the person you want them to be.

You've no doubt already discovered that efforts to change your husband or wife have ended in failure and frustration. Rather, this is a journey of exploring and demonstrating genuine love, even when your desire is dry and your motives are feeling low. The truth is, love is a decision and not just a feeling. It is selfless, sacrificial, and transformational. And when love is truly demonstrated as it was intended, your relationship is much more likely to change for the better.

Each day of this journey will contain three very important elements: First, a unique aspect of love will be discussed. Read each of these carefully and be open to a new understanding of what it means to genuinely love someone.

Second, you will be given a specific dare to do for your spouse. Some will be easy and some very challenging. But take each dare seriously, and be creative and courageous enough to attempt it. Don't be discouraged if outside situations prevent you from accomplishing a specific dare. Just pick back up as soon as you can and proceed with the journey.

Last, you will be given journal space to log what you are learning and doing and how your spouse is responding. Take advantage of this space to capture what is happening with both you and your mate. These notes will record your progress and become priceless and helpful to you in the future.

Remember, you have the responsibility to protect and guide your heart. Don't give up and don't get discouraged. Resolve to lead your heart and to make it through to the end. Learning to truly love is one of the most important things you will ever do.

Now these three remain: faith, hope, and love.
But the greatest of these is love. (1 Corinthians 13:13)

IF I SPEAK WITH THE TONGUES OF MEN AND
OF ANGELS, BUT DO NOT HAVE LOVE, I HAVE
BECOME A NOISY GONG OR A CLANGING CYMBAL.

IF I HAVE THE GIFT OF PROPHECY,
AND KNOW ALL MYSTERIES AND ALL
KNOWLEDGE; AND IF I HAVE ALL FAITH,
SO AS TO REMOVE MOUNTAINS,
BUT DO NOT HAVE LOVE, I AM NOTHING.

AND IF I GIVE ALL MY POSSESSIONS TO
FEED THE POOR, AND IF I SURRENDER MY
BODY TO BE BURNED, BUT DO NOT HAVE LOVE,
IT PROFITS ME NOTHING.

1 CORINTHIANS 13:1–3

DAY 1
Love is patient

Be completely humble and gentle; be patient,
bearing with one another in love. —Ephesians 4:2 NIV

Love works. It is life's purest and most powerful motivator and has far greater depth and meaning than most people realize. It gives courage to a coward, wisdom to a fool. It always does what is best for others and can empower us to face the greatest of problems.

Love can motivate a man to put away childish things, provide for his family, and take passionate stands for what he believes in—like crossing an ocean to fight for his country. Love can drive a woman to connect emotionally in relationships, comfort the hurting around her, protect her children, and extend her hand in kindness to those in need.

We are born with a lifelong thirst for love. Our hearts desperately need it like our lungs need oxygen. Love changes our motivation for living. Relationships become meaningful with it. No marriage is successful without it.

Love is built on two pillars that best define what it is. Those pillars are *patience* and *kindness*. All other characteristics of love are extensions of these two attributes. And that's where your dare will begin. With *patience*.

Love inspires you to become a patient person. When you choose to be patient, you respond in a positive way to a negative situation. You are *slow* to anger. You choose to have a long fuse instead of a quick temper. Rather than being restless and demanding, love helps you settle down and begin extending mercy to those around you.

No one likes to be around impatient people. Impatience overreacts in angry, foolish, regrettable ways. But the irony of anger toward a wrong is that it spawns new wrongs of its own. Anger almost never makes things better. In fact, it usually generates additional problems. It will trample on long-term relationships while reacting to short-term mishaps.

But *patience* stops problems in their tracks. More than biting your lip, more than clasping a hand over your mouth, patience takes a needed deep breath. It clears the air. It stops foolishness from whipping its scorpion tail all over the room. Patience is a choice to control your emotions rather than allowing your emotions to control you, and it shows discretion instead of returning evil for evil. It brings an internal calm to an external storm.

If your spouse offends you, do you quickly retaliate, or do you stay under control? Do you find that anger is your emotional default when treated unfairly? If so, you are spreading poison rather than medicine.

If you were to take off its mask, you'd see that anger is often an emotional reaction flowing out of our own ignorance, foolishness, or selfishness. Patience, however, makes us wise. It says, "Help me understand," instead of, "How dare you!" It doesn't rush to judgment, but puts our feelings on *pause* so that we can fully listen to what the other person is saying. It stands in the doorway where anger is clawing to burst in, but waits to see the whole picture before determining its best response. The Bible says, "He who is slow to anger has great understanding, but he who is quick-tempered exalts folly" (Proverbs 14:29).

As sure as a lack of patience will turn your home into a war zone, the practice of patience will foster peace and quiet. "A hot-tempered man stirs up strife, but the slow to anger calms a dispute" (Proverbs 15:18). Statements like these from the Bible book of Proverbs are clear principles with timeless relevance. Patience is where love meets wisdom. And every marriage needs that combination to stay healthy.

Love helps give your spouse permission to be human. It understands that everyone fails . . . daily. So when they make a mistake, it patiently chooses to give them more time than they deserve to correct it. Patience gives you the amazing ability to hold on during the tough times in your relationship rather than bailing out under the pressure.

So test yourself. How long is your fuse? How quickly do you adopt a bad attitude? Are you willing to wait with a smile? Can your spouse count on having a patient wife or husband to deal with? Can she know that locking her keys in the car will be met by your calm understanding rather than a demeaning lecture that makes her feel childish? Can he know that being found watching a football game won't automatically invite a loud-mouthed laundry list of better ways he should be spending his time?

What would the tone and volume of your home be like if you tried this biblical approach: "See that no one repays another with evil for evil, but always seek after that which is good for one another" (1 Thessalonians 5:15)?

Few of us do patience very well, and none of us does it naturally. But wise men and women will pursue it as an essential ingredient to their marriage relationships. That's a good starting point to demonstrate true love.

This Love Dare journey is a process, and the first thing you must resolve to do is to demonstrate patience on a daily basis. Think of it as a marathon, not a sprint. But it's a race worth running. Since we should never stop loving, we should never stop showing patience. It should be refreshed in supply every morning as the sun rises.

TODAY'S DARE

THE FIRST PART OF THIS DARE IS FAIRLY
SIMPLE. ALTHOUGH LOVE IS COMMUNICATED
IN A NUMBER OF WAYS, OUR WORDS OFTEN
REFLECT THE CONDITION OF OUR HEARTS. FOR
THE NEXT DAY, RESOLVE TO DEMONSTRATE
PATIENCE AND TO SAY NOTHING NEGATIVE
TO YOUR SPOUSE AT ALL. IF THE TEMPTATION
ARISES, CHOOSE NOT TO SAY ANYTHING. IT'S
BETTER TO HOLD YOUR TONGUE THAN TO SAY
SOMETHING YOU'LL REGRET.

___ Check here when you've completed today's dare.

Did anything happen today to cause anger toward your
mate? Were you tempted to think disapproving thoughts and
to let them come out in words? How did you handle that?

_____

_____

_____

_____

_____

_____

Everyone must be quick to hear, slow to speak and slow to anger. (James 1:19)

"Put your heart and soul into this, and you will see the change soon."—Elna

DAY 2
Love is kind

Be kind to one another, tender-hearted, forgiving each other, just as God in Christ also has forgiven you. —Ephesians 4:32

Kindness is love in action. If patience is how love *reacts* in order to minimize a negative circumstance, kindness is how love *acts* to maximize a positive circumstance. Patience avoids a problem; kindness creates a blessing. One is preventive, the other proactive. These two sides of love are the cornerstones on which many of the other attributes we will discuss are built.

Love makes you kind. And kindness makes you likeable. When you're kind, people want to be around you. They see you as being good *to* them and good *for* them.

The Bible keys in on the importance of kindness: "Do not let kindness and truth leave you; bind them around your neck, write them on the tablet of your heart. So you will find favor and good repute in the sight of God and man" (Proverbs 3:3–4). Kind people simply find favor wherever they go. Even at home.

But "kindness" can feel a little generic when you try defining it, much less living it. So let's break kindness down into four basic core ingredients:

Initiative. Kindness thinks ahead, then takes the first step. No request required. It doesn't sit there waiting to be prompted or coerced before getting off the couch. The kind husband or wife will be the one who greets first, smiles first, serves first, and forgives first. They don't require the other to get his or her act together before showing love. When acting from kindness, you see the need, and then you quickly make your move. First.

Gentleness. When you're operating from kindness, you're careful how you treat your spouse, never being unnecessarily callous or harsh. You're sensitive. Tender. Even if you need to say hard things, you'll bend over backwards to make your rebuke or challenge as easy to hear as possible. You speak the truth in love.

Helpfulness. Being kind means you meet the needs of the moment. If it's housework, you get busy. A listening ear? You give it. Kindness graces a wife with the ability to serve her husband without worrying about her rights. Kindness makes a husband curious to discover what his wife needs, then motivates him to be the one who steps up and ensures those needs are met—even if his are put on hold.

Willingness. Kindness inspires you to be agreeable. Instead of being obstinate, reluctant, or stubborn, you cooperate, you stay flexible. Rather than complaining or making excuses, you look for creative ways to accommodate and adjust. A kind husband ends thousands of potential arguments by his willingness to listen first rather than demand his way.

Jesus described the kindness of love in His parable of the Good Samaritan, found in the Bible—Luke, chapter 10.

A Jewish man is attacked by robbers and then left for dead on a remote road. Two religious leaders, respected among their people, walk by without choosing to stop. Too busy. Too important. Too fond of clean hands. But a common man of another race—the hated Samaritans, whose dislike for the Jews was both bitter and mutual—sees this stranger in need and is moved with compassion. Crossing all cultural boundaries and risking ridicule, he stops to help the man. Bandaging his wounds and putting him on his own donkey, he carries him to safety and pays all his medical expenses out of his own pocket. Where years of racism had caused strife and division, one act of kindness brought two enemies together. Taking the initiative, this man demonstrated true kindness in every way. Gently. Helpfully. Willingly.

Jesus illustrated how love could cause even enemies to reach out to one another in kindness. If enemies can do it, how about intimates? How might love ramp up the level of kindness in your relationships? In your marriage?

Wasn't kindness one of the key things that drew you and your spouse together in the first place? When you married, weren't you expecting to enjoy his or her kindness for the rest of your life? Didn't your mate feel the same way about you? Even though the years can take the edge off that desire, your enjoyment in marriage is still linked to the daily level of kindness expressed. It fuels mutual delight.

The Bible describes a woman whose husband and children bless and praise her. Among her noble attributes are these: "She opens her mouth in wisdom, and the teaching of kindness is on her tongue" (Proverbs 31:26). How about you? How would your husband or wife describe you on the kindness meter? How harsh are you? How gentle and helpful? Do you wait to be asked, or do you take the initiative to help? Don't wait for your spouse to be kind first. Make it your daily mission.

It is difficult to demonstrate love when you feel little to no motivation. But love in its truest sense is not based on feelings. Rather, love determines to show thoughtful actions even when there seems to be no reward. You will never learn to love until you learn to demonstrate kindness. First.

TODAY'S DARE

IN ADDITION TO SAYING NOTHING NEGATIVE TO YOUR SPOUSE AGAIN TODAY, DO AT LEAST ONE UNEXPECTED GESTURE AS AN ACT OF KINDNESS.

___ Check here when you've completed today's dare.

What discoveries about love did you make today? What specifically did you do in this dare? How did you show kindness? How can you make this a daily habit?

_____

_____

_____

_____

_____

_____

_____

_____

_____

_____

_____

_____

What is desirable in a man is his kindness. (Proverbs 19:22)

"I had forgotten how to love and be loved. I am on Day 2,
and I am beginning to see the light again."—Stacey

DAY 3
Love is not selfish

Be devoted to one another in brotherly love;
give preference to one another in honor. —Romans 12:10

Selfishness and love are in constant opposition to one another. While love asks us to deny ourselves for the sake of someone else, selfishness compels us to focus on ourselves at their expense. Selfishness is like a disease that suffocates our capacity to love. When we choose self-centeredness, we become *higher maintenance*—more needy, overly sensitive, demanding. And then when we don't get our way, we judge others harshly while being blind to our own faults.

Sadly, we live in a world that is enamored with "self." The culture around us teaches us to focus on our personal appearance, feelings, and desires as the top priority. We despise this trait in other people but justify it in ourselves. "I deserve . . ." and "I expect . . ." and "I want . . ." are appetizers we use to feed selfishness.

Regrettably, these selfish tendencies are engrained into every person from birth. You can see it in the way young children act, and often in the way adults use and mistreat one another. Almost every sinful action can be traced back to a selfish motive. And its dangers become painfully apparent once inside a marriage relationship.

Marriage exposes our selfishness in living color. When a husband puts his interests, desires, and priorities ahead of his wife, he is flying a flag of his own selfishness. When a wife constantly complains about the time and energy she spends meeting the needs of her husband, she's revealing her selfishness. Moodiness and complaining are selfishness in disguise. Laziness and irresponsibility are other masks it wears. Boasting and bragging. Being easily angered. Talking too much. Never listening. The list goes on and on. Even generous actions can be selfish if the motive is to gain bragging rights or receive a reward.

In reading this, did you focus just now on your partner's tendency to do some of these things but ignore your own? Why do we have such low standards for ourselves and yet such high expectations for our mate? The answer is a painful pill to swallow. *We all struggle with selfishness.*

The bottom line is this: you either make decisions out of love for others or love for yourself.

But love "does not seek its own" (1 Corinthians 13:5). It beautifully finds its satisfaction in the welfare of others. Loving couples in loving marriages are bent on humbling themselves and taking good care of the other flawed human with whom they have chosen to share their lives. They understand that by getting married, they are giving themselves away and releasing the right to live the rest of their lives for themselves. It's putting the happiness of their partner before their own.

Choosing to love your mate will cause you to say "no" to what you want so you can say "yes" to what they need. It doesn't mean you cannot enjoy any personal fulfillment, but you don't negate the happiness of your spouse to enjoy it yourself.

Love also leads to inner freedom. It helps liberate you from the anxiety of unrealistic expectations and unmet demands. By prioritizing the well-being of your mate, you experience a fulfillment that cannot be duplicated by selfish actions.

Unselfish people are a perpetual delight. They make amazing friends and spouses. They are willing to set their own jealousy and demands aside and lose themselves in the joy of loving, serving, and giving to another. Often this is practiced by simply allowing your mate a few seconds to go first, speak first, or be served before you are. The more you learn to resist your own selfishness daily, the stronger, more lovable, and happier you will become.

Nobody knows you as well as your spouse. And that means no one will be quicker to recognize a change when you deliberately start sacrificing your wants and wishes to make sure his or her needs are met. They may welcome it with warmth or be silently suspicious, but they will likely notice it.

If you find this day's challenge hard to swallow and are frustrated with the idea of sacrificing your own desires to benefit your spouse, then you may have a deeper problem with selfishness than you want to admit.

Ask yourself these questions:

- Do I truly want what's best for my husband or wife?
- Do I want them to feel loved by me?
- Do they believe I have their best interests in mind?
- Do they see me as looking out for myself first, or *them* first?

Remember, your partner also has the challenge of learning to love a selfish person. But don't wait on them to *earn* your love. Determine to be the first to demonstrate real love to them, with your eyes wide open. Show them what it looks like by your unexpected example. And when all is said and done, you'll both be more fulfilled.

"Do nothing from selfishness or empty conceit, but with humility of mind regard one another as more important than yourselves" (Philippians 2:3).

WHATEVER YOU PUT YOUR TIME, ENERGY, AND
MONEY INTO WILL BECOME MORE IMPORTANT
TO YOU. IT'S HARD TO CARE FOR SOMETHING
YOU ARE NOT INVESTING IN. ALONG WITH
REFRAINING FROM ANY NEGATIVE COMMENTS,
BUY YOUR SPOUSE SOMETHING THAT SAYS,
"I WAS THINKING OF YOU TODAY."

___ Check here when you've completed today's dare.

What did you choose as the gift for your spouse? What
happened when you gave it to them? What was their response?

Where jealousy and selfish ambition exist, there is disorder. (James 3:16)

_____

_____

_____

_____

_____

_____

_____

_____

_____

_____

_____

_____

_____

_____

_____

_____

_____

_____

_____

_____

_____

_____

_____

_____

_____

_____

_____

_____

_____

"For the first time in my life, I am doing things the right way.
I am really learning how to love her, and how much I love her."—Joe

Day 4
Love is thoughtful

How precious also are Your thoughts to me. . . .
How vast is the sum of them! If I should count them,
they would outnumber the sand. —Psalm 139:17–18

Love thinks. It's not a mindless feeling that rides on waves of emotion and falls asleep mentally. It keeps busy in thought, knowing that loving thoughts precede loving actions.

When you first fell in love, being thoughtful came quite naturally. You spent hours dreaming of what your loved one looked like, wondering what he or she was doing, rehearsing impressive things to say, then enjoying sweet memories of the time you spent together. You honestly confessed, "I can't stop thinking about you."

But for most couples, things begin to change after marriage. The wife finally has her man; the husband has his trophy. The hunt is over and the pursuing done. Sparks of romance slowly burn into gray embers, and the motivation for thoughtfulness cools. You drift into focusing on your job, your friends, your problems, your personal desires, yourself. After a while, you unintentionally begin to ignore the needs of your mate.

But the fact that marriage has added another person to your universe does not change. Therefore, if your thinking doesn't mature enough to constantly include this person, you catch yourself being surprised rather than being thoughtful.

"Today's our anniversary?"

"I didn't think I needed to consult you in that decision."

"Why would that upset you?"

If you don't learn to be thoughtful, you end up regretting missed opportunities to demonstrate love. Thoughtlessness is a silent enemy to a loving relationship.

Let's be honest. Men struggle with thoughtlessness more than women. A man can focus like a laser on one thing and forget the rest of the world. Whereas this can benefit him in that one arena, it can make him overlook other things that need his attention.

A woman, on the other hand, is more multi-conscious, able to maintain an amazing awareness of many factors at once. She can talk on the phone, cook, know where the kids are in the house, and wonder why her husband isn't helping . . . all simultaneously. Adding to this, a woman also tends to think relationally. When she works on something, she is cognizant of all the people who are somehow connected to it.

Both of these tendencies are examples of how God designed women to complete their men. As God said at creation, "It is not good for the man to be alone; I will make him a helper suitable for him" (Genesis 2:18). But these differences also create opportunities for misunderstanding.

Men, for example, tend to think in headlines and say exactly what they mean. Not much is needed to understand the message. His words are more literal and shouldn't be over-analyzed. But women often think and speak between the lines. They tend to hint. A man needs to listen for what is implied if he wants to get the full meaning.

If a couple doesn't understand this about one another, the fallout can result in endless disagreements. He's frustrated wondering why she speaks in riddles and doesn't just come out and say things. She's frustrated wondering why he's so inconsiderate and doesn't add two and two together and just figure her out.

A woman deeply longs for her husband to be thoughtful. It is a key to helping her feel loved. When she speaks, a wise man will listen like a detective to discover the unspoken needs and desires her words imply. If, however, she always has to put the pieces together for him, it steals the opportunity for him to demonstrate that he loves her.

This also explains why women will get upset with their husbands without telling them why. In her mind she's thinking, "I shouldn't have to spell it out for him. He should be able to look at the situation and see what's going on here." At the same time, he's grieved because he can't read her mind, and he wonders why he's being punished for a crime he didn't know he committed.

Love requires thoughtfulness—on both sides—the kind that builds bridges through the constructive combination of patience, kindness, and selflessness. Love teaches you to meet in the middle, to respect and appreciate how your spouse uniquely thinks.

A husband should listen to his wife and learn to be considerate of her unspoken messages. A wife should learn to communicate truthfully and not say one thing while meaning another. But it's easy to become angry and frustrated instead, following the destructive pattern of "ready, shoot, aim." You speak harshly now and determine later if you should have said it. But the thoughtful nature of love teaches you to engage your mind before engaging your lips. Love thinks before speaking. It filters words through a grid of truth and kindness.

When was the last time you spent a few minutes thinking about how you could better understand and demonstrate love to your spouse? What immediate need can you meet? What's the next event (anniversary, birthday, holiday) you could be preparing for? Great marriages come from great thinking.

TODAY'S DARE

CONTACT YOUR SPOUSE SOMETIME DURING
THE BUSINESS OF THE DAY. HAVE NO AGENDA
OTHER THAN ASKING HOW HE OR SHE
IS DOING AND IF THERE IS ANYTHING
YOU COULD DO FOR THEM.

__ Check here when you've completed today's dare.

What did you learn about yourself or your spouse by doing
this today? How could this become a more natural, routine,
and genuinely helpful part of your lifestyle?

I thank my God in all my remembrance of you. (Philippians 1:3)

"All I can think about now is how I can make her feel the love I have for her."—Shaun

Day 5
Love is not rude

He who blesses his friend with a loud voice early in the morning, it will be reckoned a curse to him. —Proverbs 27:14

Nothing irritates others as quickly as being rude. Rudeness is unnecessarily saying or doing things that are unpleasant for another person to be around. To be rude is to act unbecoming, embarrassing, or disrespectful. In marriage, this could be a foul mouth, poor table manners, or a habit of making sarcastic quips. Any way you look at it, no one enjoys being around a rude person. Rude behavior may seem insignificant to the person doing it, but it's unpleasant to those on the receiving end.

As always, love has something to say about this. When a man is driven by love, he intentionally behaves in a way that's more pleasant for his wife to be around. If a woman desires to love her husband, she purposefully avoids things that frustrate him or cause him discomfort.

The bottom line is: *genuine love minds its manners.*

Embracing this one concept could add some fresh air to your marriage. Good manners express to your wife or husband, "I value you enough to exercise some self-control around you. I want to be a person who's a pleasure to be with." When you allow love to change your behavior—even in the smallest of ways—you restore an atmosphere of honor to your relationship. People who practice good etiquette tend to raise the respect level of the environment and people around them.

For the most part, the etiquette you use at home is much different than the kind you employ with friends, or even with total strangers. You may be barking or pouting around the house, but if the front door chimes, you open it with a kind, welcoming smile. Yet if you dare to love, you'll also want to give your best to your own.

If you don't let love motivate you to make some needed changes in your behavior, you will unnecessarily limit the quality and enjoyment level of your marriage relationship. The more respectful and honorable your behavior, the more attractive and romantically appealing you become to your spouse.

Women tend to be much better at certain types of manners than men, since their femininity makes them naturally more gentle and elegant. Because men are drawn to people who show them respect, a woman's choice to lace her speech with respectful tones is very effective in winning her husband's heart, persuading him, and helping him to sense her love. In contrast, a wife can be very rude if she speaks down to her husband, ignores his decisions, or becomes argumentative. King Solomon said, "Better to live on a corner of the roof than share a house with a quarrelsome wife" (Proverbs 25:24 NIV).

But men especially need to learn this important lesson about manners. It is unloving to our wives to treat them like "one of the guys" rather than as a lady we have chosen to love and prize above all others. A husband shows great strength when he honors his wife by practicing self-control rather than doing whatever his feelings compel. The Bible says, "It is well with the man who is gracious" (Psalm 112:5). A man of discretion will find out what is appropriate, then adjust his behavior accordingly.

There are two main reasons why people are rude: *ignorance* and *self-centeredness*. Neither, of course, is a good thing. A child is born ignorant of etiquette, needing lots of help and training. But a simple learning of basic etiquette can greatly help them learn discretion. We adults, however, display our ignorance at another level. We know the rules, but we can be blind to how we break them or be too self-centered to care. In fact, we may not even realize how unpleasant we can be to live with at times. Test yourself with these questions:

- How does your spouse feel about the way you speak and act around them?
- How does your behavior affect your mate's sense of worth and self-esteem?
- Would your husband or wife say you're a blessing, or that you're condescending and embarrassing?

If you're thinking that your spouse—not you—is the only one who needs work in this area, you're likely suffering from an undiagnosed case of ignorance, with a secondary condition of self-centeredness. Remember, love is not rude but lifts you to a higher standard.

Do you wish your spouse would quit doing the things that bother you? Then it's time to stop doing the things that bother them. Will you be thoughtful and loving enough to discover and avoid the behaviors that can cause life to be unpleasant for your mate? Will you dare to be delightful?

Here are three guiding principles when it comes to practicing etiquette in your marriage:

1. *Guard the Golden Rule.* Treat your mate the same way you want to be treated (see Luke 6:31).
2. *No double standards.* Be as considerate to your spouse as you are to strangers, friends, and coworkers.
3. *Honor requests.* Consider what your husband or wife has already asked you to do or not do. If in doubt . . . ask.

ASK YOUR SPOUSE TO TELL YOU THREE
THINGS THAT CAUSE HIM OR HER TO BE
UNCOMFORTABLE OR IRRITATED WITH YOU.
YOU MUST DO SO WITHOUT ATTACKING THEM
OR JUSTIFYING YOUR BEHAVIOR. THIS IS
FROM THEIR PERSPECTIVE ONLY.

___ Check here when you've completed today's dare.

What things did your spouse point out about you that need
your attention? How did you handle hearing it? What do you
plan to do to improve these areas?

The words from the mouth of a wise man are gracious. (Ecclesiastes 10:12)

"I'm only five days into The Love Dare, but I can already
see a big change in myself, and I like the new me."—Chris

DAY 6
Love is not irritable

He who is slow to anger is better than the mighty, and he who rules his spirit, than he who captures a city. —Proverbs 16:32

Love is hard to offend and quick to forgive. How easily do you get irritated and offended? Some people live by the motto, "Never pass up an opportunity to get upset with your spouse." When something goes wrong, they quickly take full advantage of it by expressing how hurt or frustrated they are. But this is the opposite reaction of love.

To be *irritable* means "to be near the point of a knife." Not far from being poked. People who are irritable are locked, loaded, and ready to overreact.

When under pressure, love doesn't turn sour. Minor problems don't yield major reactions. The truth is, love does not get angry or hurt unless there is a legitimate and just reason in the sight of God. A loving husband will remain calm and patient, showing mercy and restraining his temper. Rage and violence are out of the question. A loving wife is not overly sensitive or cranky but exercises emotional self-control. She chooses to be a flower among the thorns and respond pleasantly during prickly situations.

If you are walking under the influence of love, you will be a joy, not a jerk. Ask yourself, "Am I a calming breeze, or a storm waiting to happen?"

Why do people become irritable? There are at least two key reasons that contribute to it:

First, *stress*. Stress weighs you down, drains your energy, weakens your health, and invites you to be cranky. It can be brought on by *relational* causes: arguing, division, and bitterness. There are also *excessive* causes: overworking, overplaying, and overspending. And there are *deficiencies*: not getting enough rest, nutrition, or exercise. Oftentimes we inflict these daggers on ourselves, and this sets us up to be irritable.

Life is a marathon, not a sprint. This means you must balance, prioritize, and pace yourself. Too often we throw caution to the wind and run full steam ahead, doing what feels right at the moment. Soon we are gasping for air, wound up in knots, and ready to snap. The increasing pressure can wear away at our patience and our relationships.

The Bible can help you avoid unhealthy stress. It teaches you to let love guide your relationships so you aren't caught up in unnecessary arguments (Colossians 3:12–14). To pray through your anxieties instead of tackling them on your own (Philippians 4:6–7). To delegate when you are overworked (Exodus 18:17–23). To avoid overindulgence (Proverbs 25:16).

It also exhorts you to take a "Sabbath" day every week for worship and rest. This strategically allows you time to recharge, refocus, and add margin or breathing room to your weekly schedule. By establishing these breaks and extra spaces, you will place cushions between you and the pressures around you, reducing the stress that keeps you on edge around your mate.

But there is a second, deeper reason why you become irritable—*selfishness*. When you're irritable, the heart of the problem is primarily a problem of the heart. Jesus said, "Out of the abundance of the heart the mouth speaks" (Matthew 12:34 NKJV). Some people are like lemons: when life squeezes them, they pour out a sour response. Some are more like peaches: when the pressure is on, the result is still sweet.

Being easily angered is an indicator that a hidden area of selfishness or insecurity is present where love is supposed to rule. But selfishness also wears many other masks:

Lust, for example, is the result of being ungrateful for what you have and choosing to covet or burn with passion for something that is forbidden. When your heart is lustful, it will become easily frustrated and angered (James 4:1–3). *Bitterness* takes root when you respond in a judgmental way and refuse to work through your anger. A bitter person's unresolved anger leaks out when he is provoked (Ephesians 4:31). *Greed* for more money and possessions will frustrate you with unfulfilled desires (1 Timothy 6:9–10). These strong cravings coupled with dissatisfaction lead you to lash out at anyone who stands in your way. *Pride* leads you to act harshly in order to protect your ego and reputation. Fear of embarrassment causes overreaction.

These motivations can never be satisfied. But when love enters your heart, it calms you down and inspires you to quit focusing on yourself. It loosens your grasp and helps you let go of unnecessary things.

Love will lead you to forgive instead of holding a grudge. To be grateful instead of greedy. To be content rather than rushing into more debt. Love encourages you to be happy when someone else succeeds rather than lying awake at night in envy. Love says "share the inheritance" rather than "fight with your relatives." It reminds you to prioritize your family rather than sacrifice them for a promotion at work. In each decision, love ultimately lowers your stress and helps you release the venom that can build up inside. It then sets up your heart to respond to your spouse with patience and encouragement rather than anger and exasperation.

TODAY'S DARE

CHOOSE TODAY TO START REACTING TO
TOUGH CIRCUMSTANCES IN YOUR MARRIAGE
WITH LOVE INSTEAD OF IRRITATION. BEGIN BY
MAKING A LIST BELOW OF AREAS WHERE YOU
NEED TO ADD MARGIN TO YOUR SCHEDULE.
THEN LIST ANY SELFISH MOTIVATIONS THAT
YOU NEED TO RELEASE FROM YOUR LIFE.

___ Check here when you've completed today's dare.

Where do you need to add margin to your life? When
have you recently overreacted? What was your real motivation
behind it? Consider what "good things" you might should say
"no" to so that you can be free to prioritize the "best things."
What decisions have you made today?

_____

_____

_____

_____

_____

_____

I always do my best to have a clear conscience toward God and men. (Acts 24:16)

"*This book continues to help me day by day to be patient and kind, leading my heart to love.*"—Jen

DAY 7
Love believes the best

[Love] *believes all things, hopes all things.* —*1 Corinthians 13:7*

In the deep and private corridors of your heart, there is a room. It's called the Appreciation Room. It's where your thoughts go when you encounter positive and encouraging things about your spouse. And every so often, you enjoy visiting this special place.

On the walls are written kind words and phrases describing the good attributes of your mate. These may include characteristics like "honest" and "intelligent," or phrases like "hard worker," "wonderful cook," or "beautiful eyes." They are things you've discovered about your husband or wife that have embedded themselves in your memory. When you think about these things, your appreciation for your spouse begins to increase. In fact, the more time you spend meditating on these positive attributes, the more grateful you are for your mate.

Most things in the Appreciation Room were likely written in the initial stages of your relationship. You could summarize them as things you liked and respected about your loved one. Each inscription was true, honorable, and good. And you spent a great deal of time dwelling on them in this room . . . before you were married. But you may have found that you don't visit this special room as often as you once did. That's because there is another competing room nearby.

Down another darker corridor of your heart lies the Depreciation Room, and sadly you visit there as well. On its walls are written the things that bother and irritate you most about your spouse. You placed these words and opinions there out of frustration, hurt feelings, and the disappointment of unmet expectations.

This room is lined with the weaknesses and failures of your husband or wife. Their bad habits, hurtful words, and poor decisions are written in large letters that cover the walls from one end to the other. If you stay in this room long enough, you get depressed and start expressing things like, "My wife is so selfish," or "My husband can be such a jerk." Or maybe, "I think I married the wrong person."

Some people write very hateful things in this room, where tell-off statements are rehearsed for the next argument. Emotional injuries fester here, adding more scathing remarks to the walls. It's where ammunition is kept for the next big fight and bitterness is allowed to spread like a disease. People fall out of love here.

But know this. Spending time in the Depreciation Room kills marriages. Divorces are plotted in this room and violent plans are schemed. The more time you spend in this place, the more your heart devalues your spouse. It begins the moment you walk in the door, and your care for them lessens with every second that ticks by.

You may say, "But these things are true!" Yes, but so are the things in the Appreciation Room. Everyone fails and has areas that need growth. Everyone has unresolved issues, hurts, and personal baggage. This is a sad aspect of being human. We have all sinned. But we possess this unfortunate tendency to downplay our own negative attributes while putting our partner's failures under a magnifying glass.

Let's get down to the real issue here. Love knows about the Depreciation Room and does not live in denial that it exists.

But love chooses not to live there.

You must decide to stop running to this room and lingering there after every frustrating event in your relationship. It does you no good and drains the joy out of your marriage.

Love chooses to believe the best about people. It gives them the benefit of the doubt. It refuses to fill in the unknowns with negative assumptions. And when our worst hopes are proven to be true, love makes every effort to deal with them and move forward. As much as possible, love focuses on the positive.

It's time to start thinking differently. It's time to let love lead your thoughts and your focus. The only reason you should glance in the door of the Depreciation Room is to know how to pray for your spouse. And the only reason you should ever go in this room is to write "COVERED IN LOVE" in huge letters across the walls.

It's time to move into the Appreciation Room, to settle down and make it your home. As you choose to meditate on the positives, you will learn that many more wonderful character qualities could be written across these walls. Your spouse is a living, breathing, endless book to be read. Dreams and hopes have yet to be realized. Talents and abilities may be discovered like hidden treasure. But the choice to explore them starts with a decision by you.

You must develop the habit of reining in your negative thoughts and focusing on the positive attributes of your mate. This is a crucial step as you learn to lead your heart to truly love your spouse. It is a decision that you make, whether they deserve it or not.

TODAY'S DARE

FOR TODAY'S DARE, GET TWO SHEETS
OF PAPER. ON THE FIRST ONE, SPEND
A FEW MINUTES WRITING OUT POSITIVE
THINGS ABOUT YOUR SPOUSE. THEN DO
THE SAME WITH NEGATIVE THINGS ON THE
SECOND SHEET. PLACE BOTH SHEETS IN A
SECRET PLACE FOR ANOTHER DAY. THERE IS
A DIFFERENT PURPOSE AND PLAN FOR EACH.
AT SOME POINT DURING THE REMAINDER
OF THE DAY, PICK A POSITIVE ATTRIBUTE FROM
THE FIRST LIST AND THANK YOUR SPOUSE
FOR DEMONSTRATING THIS CHARACTERISTIC.

___ Check here when you've completed today's dare.

Which list was easier to make? What did this reveal about
your thoughts? What attribute did you thank your spouse for
having?

_____

_____

_____

_____

_____

If there is anything praiseworthy—meditate on these things. (Philippians 4:8 NKJV)

*"I wasted so many years focusing a spotlight on his failings.
I missed the beautiful garden blooming all around me."*—Michelle

DAY 8
Love is not jealous

Love is as strong as death, its jealousy unyielding as the grave.
It burns like blazing fire. —Song of Solomon 8:6 NIV

Jealousy is one of the strongest drives known to man. It comes from the root word for *zeal* and means "to burn with an intense fire." The Scripture pointedly says, "Wrath is fierce and anger is a flood, but who can stand before jealousy?" (Proverbs 27:4).

There are actually two forms: a *legitimate* jealousy based on love, and an *illegitimate* jealousy based on envy. Legitimate jealousy sparks when someone you love, who belongs to you, turns his or her heart away and replaces you with someone else. If a wife has an affair and gives herself to another person, her husband may have a justified, jealous anger because of his love for her. He is longing to have back what is rightfully his.

The Bible describes God as having this kind of righteous jealousy for His people. It's not that He is envious *of* us, wishing He had what we have (since He already owns everything). It's that He deeply longs *for* us, desiring for us to keep Him as our first love. He knows that He alone is our greatest hope and will satisfy our deepest needs. So He doesn't want us to let anything take precedence over Him in our hearts. The Bible warns us not to worship anything but Him, because "the Lord your God is a consuming fire, a jealous God" (Deuteronomy 4:24).

With this concept established, we will now shift our focus to the illegitimate kind of jealousy that stands in opposition to love—the one rooted in selfishness. This is to be jealous *of* someone, to be moved with envy.

Do you struggle with being jealous of others? Your friend is more popular, so you feel hatred towards her. Your coworker gets the promotion, so you can't sleep that night. He may have done nothing wrong, but you've become bitter because of his success. It has been said that people will celebrate your level of success as long as it does not exceed theirs.

Jealousy is a common struggle. It is sparked when someone else upstages you and gets something you want. This can be very painful depending upon how selfish you are. Instead of congratulating them, you fume in anger and think ill of them. If you're not careful, jealousy slithers like a viper into your heart and strikes your motivations and relationships. It can poison you from living the life of love God intended.

If you don't diffuse your anger by learning to love others, you may eventually begin plotting against them. The Bible says that envy leads to fighting, quarreling, and every evil thing (James 3:16; 4:1–2).

There is a string of violent jealousy seen throughout Scripture. It caused the first murder when Cain despised God's acceptance of his brother's offering. Sarah sent away her handmaiden because Hagar could bear children while Sarah could not. Joseph's brothers discovered he was their father's favorite, so they threw him in a pit and sold him as a slave. Jesus was more loving, powerful, and popular than the chief priests, so they envied Him and plotted His betrayal and crucifixion.

You don't usually get jealous of disconnected strangers. The ones you're tempted to be jealous of are primarily in the same arena with you. They work in your office, play in your league, run in your circles . . . or live in your house. Yes, if you aren't careful, jealousy can also infect your marriage.

When you were married, you were given the role of becoming your spouse's biggest cheerleader and the captain of his or her fan club. Both of you became *one* in life and were to share in the enjoyment of the other. But if selfishness rules, any good thing happening to only one of you can be a catalyst for envy rather than congratulations.

He may be enjoying golf on the weekend while she stays home cleaning the house. He boasts to her about shooting a great score, and she feels like shooting *him*.

Or perhaps she is constantly invited to go out with friends while he is left at home with the dog. If he's not careful, he can resent her popularity, while she resents his loyalty to the dog.

Because love is not selfish and puts others first, it refuses to let jealousy in. It leads you to celebrate the successes of your spouse rather than resenting them. A loving husband doesn't mind his wife being better at something, having more fun, or getting more applause. He sees her as completing him, not competing with him.

When he receives praise, he publicly thanks her for her support in aiding his own success. He refuses to brag in such a way that may cause her to resent him. A loving wife will be the first to cheer for her man when he wins. She does not compare her weaknesses to his strengths. She throws a celebration, not a pity party.

It is time to let love, humility, and gratefulness destroy any jealousy that springs up in your heart. It's time to let your mate's successes draw you closer together and give you greater opportunities to start the music and throw the confetti.

TODAY'S DARE

DETERMINE TO BECOME YOUR SPOUSE'S
BIGGEST FAN AND TO REJECT ANY THOUGHTS
OF JEALOUSY. TO HELP YOU SET YOUR HEART
ON YOUR SPOUSE AND FOCUS ON THEIR
ACHIEVEMENTS, TAKE YESTERDAY'S LIST
OF NEGATIVE ATTRIBUTES AND DISCREETLY
BURN IT. THEN SHARE WITH YOUR SPOUSE
HOW GLAD YOU ARE ABOUT A SUCCESS OR
BLESSING HE OR SHE RECENTLY ENJOYED.

___ Check here when you've completed today's dare.

How hard was it to destroy the list? What are some positive experiences that you can celebrate in the life of your mate? How can you encourage them toward future successes?

Rejoice with those who rejoice, and weep with those who weep. (Romans 12:15)

"I never dreamed I would learn so much about myself along the way."—Cheryl

DAY 9
Love makes good impressions

Greet one another with a kiss of love. —*1 Peter 5:14*

Kings bow while soldiers salute. Acquaintances wave while friends shake hands. And families embrace while lovers kiss. Greetings provide us with dynamic ways to encounter one another and show appropriate affection and respect. Each greeting depends upon the nature and closeness of each relationship.

Did you know that you can tell a lot about the current status of a couple's marriage by the way they greet one another? You can see it in her smile, hear it in his voice, and sense it in the tenderness of their touch. Or lack thereof.

A greeting can be a litmus test for relational health. Think about it: What do you and your mate reveal about your relationship, simply by how you greet one another? Is it caring? Or is it callous? Do your greetings cause your spouse to look forward to seeing you?

Some people don't greet warmly because they feel insincere. They claim, "I'm being true to how I feel inside." But there are many good reasons to be kind even when feelings are contrary—*love* being the greatest reason of all. While greetings can reflect what's currently happening in a relationship, they can also become a loving investment in its future health.

Throughout history, the Jewish people demonstrated an understanding of the power of an effective greeting. Used more than two hundred times in the Bible, the word *shalom* (meaning peace or tranquility) was a word intentionally employed to greet others. They used it to say, "Have a long life, peace be to you,

and peace be to your house, and peace be to all that you have"
(1 Samuel 25:6). This word, still used today, reveals how a daily
greeting can be turned into a dynamic blessing.

You don't have to say "Shalom" when greeting your mate,
but sharing a strong, five-second greeting each day with your
spouse can become a long-term blessing to your relationship.
Your greeting should say, "You are priceless to me," rather than,
"You are tolerated by me."

Jesus noted that even pagans speak kindly to people they
like. That's easy for anyone to do. But God's children, He said,
are meant to be humble and gracious enough to address even
their enemies with kindness.

This raises the question: How do you greet your friends,
coworkers, and neighbors? How about acquaintances you see
in public? You may even encounter someone you don't necessarily like and yet still acknowledge them out of courtesy.

So if you're this polite to others, doesn't your spouse
deserve the same? Times ten?

It can be as simple as what you say when you wake up in
the morning, the look on your face when you get in the car,
the energy in your voice when you're on the phone. Consider
the difference it would make in your spouse's day if everything
about you expressed the fact that you were really, really glad to
see them.

A good greeting sets the stage for positive, healthy interaction. Like love, it makes a person feel valued and puts wind in
their sails for better moments ahead.

Think back to the story Jesus told of the prodigal son. This
young, rebellious man demanded his inheritance money and
then wasted it on a foolish lifestyle. But soon his poor choices
caught up with him, and he found himself eating scraps in
a pigpen. Humbled and ashamed, he practiced his apologies

before going home to face his father. But the greeting he anticipated was not the one he received. "While he was still a long
way off, his father saw him and felt compassion for him, and
ran and embraced him and kissed him" (Luke 15:20).

This greeting was likely the last thing the son expected.
But how do you think it made him feel to receive his father's
embrace and hear his thankful tone? Overwhelmed. Deeply
loved. Treasured again. What do you think it did to their
relationship?

What kind of greetings would cause your mate to feel like
that? How could you excite his or her senses with a kinder
word, a more affectionate touch, and a more gracious tone
of voice? A loving greeting is a gift you can give your spouse
every day by what they see, hear, and feel. It is priceless in
value while costing you nothing.

Think of the opportunities you're given to greet each other
on a regular basis. When coming in the door. When meeting
for lunch. When saying goodnight. When talking or texting on
the phone. It doesn't have to be bold and dramatic every time.
But adding warmth and enthusiasm gives you the chance to
touch your mate's heart in unexpected ways.

Countless widows and widowers could tell us with tears
in their eyes what it would mean for them to have one more
chance to greet, kiss, and hold their spouses again. Since we
each have no guarantee of tomorrow, every new day with our
spouse is a gift from God for us to cherish and enjoy.

Think about your greeting. Do you use it well? Does your
spouse feel appreciated? Do they feel loved? Even when you're
not getting along too well, you can lessen the tension and help
turn things around by the way you bless them when you greet
them. Remember, love is a choice. So choose to love them at
"Hello!"

THINK OF A SPECIFIC WAY YOU'D LIKE TO
GREET YOUR SPOUSE TODAY. DO IT WITH
A SMILE AND WITH ENTHUSIASM. THEN
DETERMINE TO CHANGE YOUR GREETING
TO DAILY REFLECT MORE LOVE FOR THEM.

___ Check here when you've completed today's dare.

When and where did you choose to do your special greeting? How did your mate respond to it? How will you change
your greeting from this point on?

For I have come to have much joy and comfort in your love. (Philemon 7)

"I intend to see this through and change myself for her and our marriage."—Steve

DAY 10
Love is unconditional

God demonstrates His own love toward us, in that while
we were yet sinners, Christ died for us. —Romans 5:8

If someone were to ask you, "Why do you love your wife?"
or "Why do you love your husband?"—what would you say?

Most men would mention their wife's beauty, her sense of
humor, her kindness, or her inner strength. They might talk
about her cooking, her knack for decorating, or what a good
mother she is.

Women would probably say something about their husband's good looks or his personality. They'd commend him for
his steadiness and consistent character. They'd say they love
him because he's always there for them. He's generous. He's
helpful.

But what if over the course of years, your wife or husband
stopped being every one of these things. Would you still love
them? Based on your answers above, the only logical response
would be "no." If your reasons for loving your spouse all have
something to do with his or her qualities—and then those
same qualities suddenly or gradually disappear—your basis for
love is over. The only way love can last a lifetime is if it's unconditional. The truth is: lasting love is not determined by the one
being loved but rather by the one *choosing* to love.

The Bible refers to this kind of love by using the Greek
word *agape* (pronounced *uh*-GOP-*ay*). It differs from other
types of love, like—*phileo* (friendship) and *eros* (sexual love).
Both friendship and sex have an important place in marriage,
of course, and are a big part of the house you build together as

husband and wife. But if your marriage totally depends on having common interests or enjoying a healthy sex life, then the foundation of your relationship is unstable.

Phileo and *eros* are more responsive in nature and can fluctuate based upon feelings. When someone says, "I've fallen in love with you," it is *phileo* or *eros* love. These are fickle and can change depending upon circumstances.

It is important to recognize that it's possible to allow yourself to "fall in and out of love" with multiple people throughout life. That's why we should guard our hearts from others, guarding it for our spouse alone.

You can also fall in and out of love with your own spouse hundreds of times throughout your life, depending on how well you're getting along and how much you're investing in the relationship. Feeling "in love" is something you can enjoy and continue to rekindle over the years. But it should not determine your commitment level to your marriage.

Agape love, on the other hand, is unselfish, unconditional, and unstoppable. It is based upon choice and commitment, not feelings. So unless this kind of love forms the foundation of your marriage, the wear and tear of time could destroy it. *Agape* love is "in sickness and health" love, "for richer or poorer" love, "for better or worse" love. It is the only kind of love that is *lasting, unchanging, true* love.

That's because this is God's kind of love. He doesn't love us because we are lovable, but because He is so loving. "In this is love, not that we loved God, but that He loved us and sent His Son to be the propitiation for our sins" (1 John 4:10). If He insisted that we prove ourselves worthy of His love, we would fail miserably. But His love is a choice He makes completely on His own. It's something we receive from Him and then share with others. "We love, because He first loved us" (1 John 4:19).

If a man says to his wife, "I no longer love you," he is actually saying, "I never loved you unconditionally to begin with." His love was based on feelings or circumstances rather than commitment. That's the result of building a marriage on *phileo* or *eros* love. There must be a stronger foundation than mere friendship or sexual attraction. Unconditional love, *agape* love, will not be swayed by time or circumstance.

That's not to say that love which began for the wrong reasons cannot be restored and redeemed. In fact, when you rebuild your marriage with *agape* as its foundation, the friendship and romantic aspects of your love become more endearing than ever before. When your enjoyment of each other as both best friends and lovers is based on unwavering commitment, you will experience an intimacy that cannot be achieved any other way.

But you will struggle and ultimately fail to attain this kind of marriage unless you first allow God to begin establishing and growing His love within you. Love that "bears all things, believes all things, hopes all things, endures all things" (1 Corinthians 13:7) does not come from within. It can only come from God (1 John 4:7–16).

The Scriptures say that "neither death, nor life, nor angels, nor principalities, nor things present, nor things to come, nor powers, nor height, nor depth, nor any other created thing, will be able to separate us from the love of God, which is in Christ Jesus our Lord" (Romans 8:38–39). This is God's kind of love. And thankfully—by your choice—it can become *your* kind of love. But first you must receive it and share it.

And then, regardless of circumstances and feelings, you and your spouse can begin living confidently and securely under its shade. You will no longer say, "I love you because . . ." You will now say, "I love you, period."

TODAY'S DARE

DO SOMETHING OUT OF THE ORDINARY TODAY
FOR YOUR SPOUSE—SOMETHING THAT PROVES
(TO YOU AND TO THEM) THAT YOUR LOVE IS
BASED ON YOUR CHOICE AND NOTHING ELSE.
WASH HER CAR. CLEAN THE KITCHEN. BUY HIS
FAVORITE DESSERT. FOLD THE LAUNDRY.
DEMONSTRATE LOVE TO THEM FOR THE SHEER
JOY OF BEING THEIR PARTNER IN MARRIAGE.

___ Check here when you've completed today's dare.

Has your love typically been based on your spouse's attributes and behavior, or have you based it instead on your own commitment? How can you continue to show love when it's not returned in a way you hoped for?

_____

_____

_____

_____

_____

_____

_____

He who trusts in the Lord, lovingkindness shall surround him. (Psalm 32:10)

"We both promised if we ever fall off track, we will both do the
Love Dare all over again."—Michele

Day 11
Love cherishes

Husbands ought also to love their own wives
as their own bodies. —Ephesians 5:28

Consider these two scenarios.

A man's older car begins having serious trouble, so he takes it to a mechanic. After an assessment is made, he is told it will need a complete overhaul, which would tax his limited budget. Because of the expensive repairs, he determines to get rid of the car and spend his funds on a new vehicle. Seems reasonable, right?

Another man, an engineer, accidentally crushes his hand in a piece of equipment. He rushes to the hospital and has it x-rayed, finding that numerous bones are broken. Although frustrated and in pain, he willingly uses his savings to have it doctored and placed in a cast, then gingerly nurses it back to health over the following months. This, too, probably seems reasonable to you.

The problem within our culture is that marriage is more often treated like the first scenario. A *discardable* possession. When your relationship experiences difficulty, you are urged to dump your spouse for a "newer model." But those who have this view do not understand the significant bond between a husband and wife. The truth is, marriage is more like the second scenario. You are a part of one another. You would never cut off your hand if it was injured but would pay whatever you could afford for the best medical treatment possible. That's because your hand is priceless to you. It is part of who you are.

And so is your mate. Marriage is a beautiful mystery created by God, joining two lives together as one. This not only happens physically but spiritually and emotionally. You start off sharing the same house, the same bed, the same last name. Your identity as individuals has been joined into one. When you find success at your job, both of you rejoice. When one of you goes through a tragedy, both of you feel it. But somewhere along the way, you experience disappointment and pain. Your relationship gets broken. The sobering reality that you married a very imperfect person sets in.

This, however, does not change the fact that your spouse is still a part of you. Ephesians 5:28–29 says, "Husbands ought also to love their own wives as their own bodies. He who loves his own wife loves himself; for no one ever hated his own flesh, but nourishes and cherishes it."

The word *cherish* means "to make warm." Imagine a newborn baby who feels alone, cold, hungry, and afraid, longing to be held. Then his new mother lovingly picks him up, nursing, caressing, and holding her infant child (1 Thessalonians 2:7). Her careful attention and tender affection warms her baby both physically and emotionally. This is the biblical picture of how a husband and wife are to *cherish* one another.

Life is cold and unpredictable. Everyday stress can wear us down. Relationships can sometimes be hard and go through seasons of winter instead of those warm days of spring. It is our responsibility, above every other person on the face of the earth, to step in and tenderly touch, caress, and warm the life and the heart of our spouse.

Much of this *cherishing* can be done in how we gently touch our mate in nonsexual ways. Coming up behind your wife at the sink and kissing her on the neck. Reaching over in the car and caressing his arm. Putting your arm around her while sitting in church. Walking closely beside him and taking his hand. Holding her while you watch a movie together. Nourishing them with the warmth of your affection. Remember, when you show love to your spouse, you are showing love to yourself as well.

But there is a flip side to this coin. When you mistreat your mate, you are also mistreating yourself. Think about it. Your lives are now interwoven together. Your spouse cannot experience joy or pain, blessing or cursing, without it also affecting you. So when you attack your mate, it is like attacking your own body.

It's time to let love change your thinking. It's time for you to realize that your spouse is as much a part of you as your hand, your eye, or your heart. She, too, needs to be loved and cherished. And if she has brokenness and issues causing pain or frustration, then you should nourish and cherish her with the same love and tenderness as you would a bodily injury. If he is wounded in some way, you should think of yourself as an instrument that helps bring warmth and healing to his life.

In light of this, think about how you treat your spouse's physical body. Do you cherish it as your own? Do you treat it with respect and tenderness? Do you take pleasure in who they are? Or do you make them feel foolish or embarrassed? Just as you guard the safety and well-being of your own body, you should treasure every part of your spouse as a priceless gift.

Whenever a husband looks into the eyes of his wife, he should remember that "he who loves his wife loves himself." And a wife should remember that when she loves him, she is also giving love and honor to herself.

When you look at your mate, you're looking at a part of you. So treat her well. Speak highly of him. Nourish and cherish the love of your life.

TODAY'S DARE

HOW CAN YOU WARM THE HEART OF YOUR SPOUSE TODAY? LOOK FOR OPPORTUNITIES TO BRING WARMTH TO THE COLDNESS IN HIS OR HER LIFE. IF POSSIBLE, GIVE THEM AN UNEXPECTED, TENDER TOUCH. CHOOSE A GESTURE THAT SAYS, "I CHERISH YOU." AND DO IT WITH SINCERITY.

___ Check here when you've completed today's dare.

How did you choose to show that you cherish your mate? What did you learn from this experience?

Answering him, Jesus said, "What do you want Me to do for you?" (Mark 10:51)

"*Some dares seemed almost impossible at first, but the reward has been so much greater than the risks and setbacks.*"—Nadine

DAY 12
Love lets the other win

*Do not merely look out for your own personal interests,
but also for the interests of others.* —Philippians 2:4

If you were asked to name three areas where you and your
spouse disagree, you'd likely be able to do it without thinking
very hard. You might even be able to produce a top ten list if
given a few more minutes. And sadly, unless someone at your
house starts doing some giving in, these same issues are going
to keep popping up between you and your mate.

Sadly, stubbornness comes as a standard feature on both
husband and wife models. Defending your rights and opinions
is a foundational part of your nature and makeup. It's detrimen-
tal, though, inside a marriage relationship, and it steals away
time and productivity. It can also cause great frustration for
both of you.

Granted, being stubborn is not always bad. Some things are
worth standing up for and protecting. Our priorities, morals,
and obedience to God should be guarded with great effort. But
too often we debate over piddling things, like the color of wall
paint or the choice of restaurants.

Other times, of course, the stakes are much higher. One
of you would like more children; the other doesn't. One of you
wants to vacation with your extended family; the other doesn't.
One of you prefers home-schooling your kids; the other
doesn't. One of you thinks it's time for marriage counseling or
to get more involved in a church, while the other doesn't.

Though these issues may not crop up every day, they keep
resurfacing and don't really go away. You never seem to get any

closer to a resolution or compromise. The heels just keep digging in. It's like driving with the parking brake on.

There's only one way to get beyond stalemates such as these, and that's by finding a word that's the opposite of *stubbornness*—a word we first met while discussing kindness. That word is *willing*. It's an attitude and spirit of cooperation that should permeate our conversations. It's like a palm tree by the ocean that endures the greatest winds because it knows how to gracefully bend. And the one best example of it is Jesus Christ, as described in Philippians 2:5–11. Follow the progression of His selfless love . . .

As God, He had every right to refuse becoming a man, yet He yielded and did—because He was willing. He had the right to be served by all mankind but came to serve us instead. He had the right to live in peace and safety but willingly laid down His life for our sins. He was even willing to endure the grueling torture of the cross. He loved, cooperated, and was willing to do His Father's will instead of His own.

In light of this amazing testimony, the Bible applies to us a one-sentence summary statement: "Have this attitude in yourselves which was also in Christ Jesus" (Philippians 2:5)— the attitude of willingness, flexibility, and humble submission. It means laying down for the good of others what you have the right to claim for yourself.

All it takes for your present arguments to continue is for both of you to stay entrenched and unbending. But the very moment one of you says, "I'm willing to go your way on this one," the argument will be over. And though the follow-through may cost you a few moments of pride and discomfort, you have made a loving, lasting investment in your marriage.

"Yes, but then I'll look foolish. I'll lose the fight. I'll lose control." Well, you've already looked foolish if you have been bull-headed and refused to listen. You've already lost the fight by making this issue more important than your marriage and your spouse's sense of worth. You may have already lost emotional control by saying things that got personal and hurt your mate.

The wise and loving thing to do is to start approaching your disagreements with a willingness to not always insist on your own way. That's not to say your mate is necessarily right or being wise about a matter, but you are choosing to give strong consideration to their preference as a way of valuing them. In fact, your willingness to reconsider may cause them to loosen their resistance to you and reconsider as well.

Love's best advice comes from the Bible, which says, "The wisdom that is from above is first pure, then peaceable, gentle, willing to yield" (James 3:17 NKJV). Instead of treating your wife or husband like an enemy or someone to be guarded against, start by treating them as your closest, most honored friend. Give their words full weight.

No, you won't always see eye-to-eye. You're not supposed to be carbon copies of each other. If you were, one of you would be unnecessary. Two people who always share the same opinions and perspectives won't have any balance or flavor to enhance the relationship. Rather, your differences are for listening to and learning from.

Are you willing to bend to demonstrate love to your spouse? Or are you refusing to give in because of pride? If it doesn't matter in the long run—especially in eternity—then giving up your rights will be a loving way to bring delight and honor to the one you love. It will likely be good for you and for your marriage. Surrendering a battle may actually be the best way to greater victory.

TODAY'S DARE

DEMONSTRATE LOVE BY WILLINGLY
CHOOSING TO GIVE IN TO AN AREA OF
DISAGREEMENT BETWEEN YOU AND
YOUR SPOUSE. TELL THEM YOU ARE
PUTTING THEIR PREFERENCE FIRST.

___ Check here when you've completed today's dare.

What issue did you choose? What did giving in cost you?
How will this help you in the future?

_____

_____

_____

_____

_____

_____

_____

_____

_____

_____

If possible, so far as it depends on you, be at peace with all men. (Romans 12:18)

_____

_____

_____

_____

_____

_____

_____

_____

_____

_____

_____

_____

_____

_____

_____

_____

_____

_____

_____

_____

_____

_____

_____

"I have absolutely enjoyed the peace in my heart that comes from knowing the anger I felt for so long is gone."—Roberta

Day 13
Love fights fair

If a house is divided against itself, that house will not be able to stand.
—Mark 3:25

Like it or not, conflict in marriage is simply inevitable. When you tied the knot as bride and groom, you joined not only your hopes and dreams but also your hurts, fears, imperfections, and emotional baggage. From the moment you unpacked from your honeymoon, you began the real process of unpacking one another, unpleasantly discovering how sinful and selfish each of you could be.

Pretty soon your mate started to slip off your lofty pedestal, and you off of theirs. The forced closeness of marriage began stripping away your public façades, exposing your private problems and secret habits. Welcome to fallen humanity.

At the same time, the storms of life began testing and revealing what you're really made of. Work demands, health issues, in-law arguments, and financial needs flared up in varying degrees, adding pressure and heat to the relationship. This set the stage for disagreements to break out between the two of you. You argued and fought. You hurt. You experienced conflict. Every couple goes through it. It's par for the course. You are not alone. But not every couple survives it.

So don't think living out today's dare will drive all conflict from your marriage. Instead, this is about dealing with conflict in such a way that you come out healthier on the other side.

Both of you. Together.

The deepest, most heartbreaking damage you'll ever do (or ever have done) to your marriage will most likely occur in the thick of conflict. That's because this is when your pride is strongest. Your anger is hottest. You're the most selfish and judgmental. Your words contain the most venom. You make the worst decisions. A great marriage on Monday can start driving off the cliff on Tuesday if unbridled conflict takes over and neither of you has your foot on the brakes.

But love steps in and changes things. Love reminds you that your marriage is too valuable to allow it to self-destruct, and that your love for your spouse is more important than whatever you're fighting about. Love helps you install air bags and set up guardrails in your relationship. It protects your oneness. It reminds you that conflict can actually be turned around for good and can result in even greater unity, not less. Married couples who learn to work wisely through their conflict tend to be much closer, more trusting, more intimate, and enjoy a much deeper connection afterwards.

But how? The wisest way is to learn to fight clean by establishing healthy rules of engagement. If you don't have guidelines for how you'll approach hot topics, you won't stay in bounds when the action heats up.

Basically there are two types of boundaries for dealing with conflict: "we" boundaries and "me" boundaries.

"We" boundaries are rules you both agree on beforehand that apply during any fight or altercation. And each of you has the right to gently but directly enforce them if these rules are violated. These could include:

1. We will never mention divorce.
2. We will not bring up old, unrelated items from the past.
3. We will never fight in public or in front of our children.
4. We will call a "time out" if the conflict escalates to a damaging level.

5. We will never touch one another in a harmful way.

6. We will never go to bed angry with one another.

7. Failure is not an option. Whatever it takes, we will work this out.

"Me" boundaries are rules you personally practice on your own. Here are some of the most effective examples:

1. I will listen first before speaking. "Everyone must be quick to hear, slow to speak and slow to anger" (James 1:19). The one who listens first consistently has the advantage in a fight. You should always approach sensitive issues by respectfully asking questions rather than making assumptions or unleashing accusations.

2. I will deal with my own issues up-front. "Why do you look at the speck that is in your brother's eye, but do not notice the log that is in your own eye?" (Matthew 7:3). If you quickly admit where you were wrong and apologize first, you disarm your spouse and neutralize the ammo they were using against you while leading the way for them to deal with their mistakes as well.

3. I will speak gently and keep my voice down. "A gentle answer turns away wrath, but a harsh word stirs up anger" (Proverbs 15:1). People tend to mirror their enemy in a fight. The more intense you get, the more intense they get. The more humble and tender you become, the more humble and tender they become. Let how you are speaking be laced with love regardless of what you are saying.

Fighting fair means changing your weapons. Disagreeing with dignity. Building a bridge instead of burning one down. Love is not a fight, but it is always worth fighting for.

TALK WITH YOUR SPOUSE ABOUT
ESTABLISHING HEALTHY RULES OF
ENGAGEMENT. IF YOUR MATE IS NOT READY
FOR THIS, THEN WRITE OUT YOUR OWN
PERSONAL RULES TO "FIGHT" BY. RESOLVE
TO ABIDE BY THEM WHEN THE NEXT
DISAGREEMENT OCCURS.

___ Check here when you've completed today's dare.

If your spouse participated with you, what was their
response? What rules did you write for yourself?

_____

_____

_____

_____

_____

_____

_____

_____

Be of the same mind toward one another. (Romans 12:16)

"I needed to make changes in me if I wanted to see better results with him."—Jaime

Day 14
Love takes delight

Enjoy life with the wife you love all the days of your fleeting life.
—Ecclesiastes 9:9 HCSB

The world is constantly trying to tell you what's attractive and what's not. What's undesirable and what's hot. They peddle the latest products worn by models and movie stars hoping you will wield your wallet and credit cards. But if you embrace their unrealistic standards of beauty—of size and shape and height and weight—you will spend your whole life never content with what you see in the mirror and always wishing your spouse looked more like the photos in highly airbrushed ads.

The good news is that you don't have to waste your life chasing fantasy. You, not the rest of the world, get to determine what is most attractive and appealing to you. You can choose to enjoy and take overwhelming delight right now in the priceless treasure God has already given you in your mate. Inside and out. Nothing is stopping you. And you should!

One of the most important things you should learn on your Love Dare journey is that you should not just *follow* your heart, you should *lead* it. Don't let your feelings and emotions do the driving. You put them in the back seat and tell them where you're going.

Newlyweds *feel* their love. They take delight in the one they now call their spouse. Their affections are fresh and young, and the hope of a romantic future lives in their hearts. However, you can have something just as powerful as that fresh, new love. It comes from the *decision* to delight in your spouse and to love him or her no matter how long you've been married. In other words, love that *chooses* to love is just as beautiful as love that *feels* like loving. In many ways, it is a truer love because it has its eyes wide open.

The Scripture says that God chose to set His love on His own people even though they lacked the size or merit of other nations (Deuteronomy 7:7–8). We must do the same.

Left to selfishness and emotion, we'll always lean toward comparing the weaknesses of our spouse to the strengths of other men or women. We'll think, "My wife is not as respectful and radiant," or "My husband's not as kind and considerate." But our days are too short to waste focusing on the shadows when we could be enjoying the sunshine.

Instead, it's time to lead your heart to, once again, *delight* in your mate. To decide that the person God uniquely made them to be is who you are choosing to love and enjoy. To prize their uniqueness and remember again why you fell in love with his eyes or her personality. To take her hand and seek her companionship. To desire his conversation. To accept this person— quirks and all—and to welcome him or her back into your heart. The Bible does not say a man should marry the woman he loves, but should love the woman he marries.

It's not like you're born with certain preferences you're destined to operate from. You get to choose what you treasure. So if you're ungrateful and disapproving, it's because you choose to be. If you pick at your mate more than you praise them, it's because you've allowed selfishness in your heart to take over. You've *led* yourself into criticism.

So lead your heart back out. Learn to delight in your spouse again. When you reset your love on your spouse and reinvest the needed time and energy back into the relationship, you can watch your heart daily enjoy more of who they are.

The Bible contains many romantic love stories, none more provocative than all eight chapters from the Song of Solomon. Listen to the way these two lovers take pleasure in one another in this poetic book—

The woman: "Like an apple tree among the trees of the forest, so is my beloved among the young men. In his shade I took great delight and sat down, and his fruit was sweet to my taste. He has brought me to his banquet hall, and his banner over me is love" (Song of Solomon 2:3–4).

The man: "Arise, my darling, my beautiful one, and come along! O my dove, in the clefts of the rock, in the secret place of the steep pathway, let me see your form, let me hear your voice; for your voice is sweet, and your form is lovely" (Song of Solomon 2:13–14).

Too sappy? Too mushy? Not for those who lead their heart to delight in their beloved—even when the new wears off, even when she's wearing rollers in her hair, even when his hair is falling out. It's time to enjoy again. To laugh and flirt again. To dream again. Delightfully.

Today's dare may be directing you to a real and radical change. For some, the move toward delight may only be a small step away. For others, it may require a giant leap from ongoing disgust. But if you've been delighted before—which you were when you first got married—you can be delighted again, even if it's been a long time, even if a whole lot has happened to change your perceptions. The responsibility is yours to relearn what you love about the one to whom you've promised forever.

TODAY'S DARE

PURPOSEFULLY NEGLECT AN ACTIVITY YOU WOULD NORMALLY DO SO YOU CAN SPEND QUALITY TIME WITH YOUR SPOUSE. DO SOMETHING HE OR SHE WOULD LOVE TO DO OR A PROJECT THEY'D REALLY LIKE TO WORK ON. MAKE THE CHOICE TO ENJOY YOUR TIME TOGETHER.

___ Check here when you've completed today's dare.

What did you decide to give up? What did you do together? How did it go? What new thing did you learn (or relearn) about your spouse?

To find out more about "leading your heart," see the Appendix, page 201.

Give me your heart . . . and let your eyes delight in my ways. (Proverbs 23:26)

DAY 15
Love is honorable

*You husbands . . . live with your wives in an understanding way . . .
and show her honor as a fellow heir of the grace of life.* —1 Peter 3:7

Who is the one person you respect more than anyone in
the world? What would it mean to you if you could meet that
person for a meal or spend a day with them? You'd no doubt
feel very privileged. When they talked, you would listen with
great attentiveness. If they made a request, you would take it
very seriously and ensure it was fulfilled.

Welcome to the definition of the word *honor*.

To honor someone means to give them respect and high
esteem, to treat them as being special and of great worth. When
you speak to them, you choose your words carefully. You are
more courteous and polite. When they speak to you, you give
their words valuable weight and significance. You willingly go
the extra mile to accommodate them if at all possible, simply
out of respect for who they are. Out of *honor*. It's a noble word
that describes the noble way we should live.

The Bible speaks often of honor. We are told to "honor"
our father and mother, as well as those in authority. Husbands
are told to show "honor" to their wives (1 Peter 3:7), and wives
to show respect to their husbands (Ephesians 5:33). This is a
fundamental key to the health and strength of your marriage.
We are not told to honor our spouse only if they deserve it, but
because honoring them is right in God's sight and because of
their special position in our lives.

Honoring your mate means giving him or her your full
attention, not talking to them from behind a newspaper or

with one eye on the television. When decisions are being made that affect both of you, you give your mate's voice and opinion valuable influence in your mind. You strongly consider what they have to say. They matter—and because of the way you treat them, they should know it.

But there's another word related to *honor* that calls us to a higher place, a word that isn't often equated with marriage, though its relevance cannot be understated. It actually forms the basis for honor. That word is *holy*.

To say your mate should be "holy" to you doesn't mean that he or she is perfect. Holiness means they are set apart for a higher purpose—no longer common or everyday but extremely special and unique. A person who has become holy to you has a place no one can rival in your heart. He or she is sacred to you, a person to be *more* honored, praised, and defended.

A bride treats her wedding dress this way. After wearing it on her special day, she covers and protects it, then sets it apart from everything else in her wardrobe. You won't catch her in it when she's working in the yard or going out on the town. Her wedding dress has a value all its own. In this way, it is holy and sacred to her.

When two people marry, each spouse becomes "holy" to each other by way of "holy matrimony." This means no other person in the whole world is supposed to enjoy this level of commitment and endearment from you. Your relationship is like no other. You each commit to sharing physical intimacy with only her, only him. You establish a home with this person. You bear your children with this person. Your heart, possessions, and life are to be beautifully interwoven in the uncommon bond you share with this one individual. This is by God's design and should be your daily goal and desire.

Is that the way it is in your marriage? Would your husband

say you honor and respect him? Do you consider your wife to be set apart and highly prized? Holy?

Perhaps you *don't* feel this way—and maybe for good reason, you think. Perhaps you wish some outsider could see the level of disrespect you get from your wife or husband. You may wish to expose and blame your spouse for your own attitudes that have started to sour.

But that's not the issue with love. Love positively acts; it doesn't negatively react. Love rises above the cloudy circumstances and soars above the storm. It defies common, self-centered logic. It chooses to honor even when it's rejected. Love treats its beloved as special and sacred even when an ungrateful attitude is all it gets in return. It refuses to be pulled back into the hole of self-centered living.

It's marvelous, of course, when a husband and wife are joined in this purpose, when they're following the biblical command to be "devoted to one another" in love, when they're giving "preference to one another in honor" (Romans 12:10). "Marriage should be honored by all," the Bible says, "and the marriage bed kept pure" (Hebrews 13:4 NIV).

But when your attempts at honor go unreciprocated, you are to be honorable just the same, seeking ways to give honor to your mate. That's what love dares to do—to say, "Of all the relationships I have, I will value ours the most. Of all the people for whom I'm willing to sacrifice, I will sacrifice the most for you. With all your failures, sins, mistakes, and faults—past and present—I still choose the God-honoring way to a better marriage and a better life. I choose to love and honor you."

That's how you create an atmosphere in your marriage for love to be rekindled. That's how you lead dishonor out the door and then lead your heart to truly love your mate again.

That's the beauty of honor.

CHOOSE TO BEGIN SHOWING GREATER
HONOR TO YOUR SPOUSE ABOVE YOUR
NORMAL TENDENCY. BEGIN BY LISTENING
MORE ATTENTIVELY AND RESPECTFULLY TO
YOUR HUSBAND OR WIFE. LET YOUR MATE
SEE HOW YOU GIVE GREATER WEIGHT TO
THEIR WORDS AND REQUESTS. SHOW THAT HE
OR SHE IS RECEIVING HIGHER ESTEEM
IN YOUR EYES THAN BEFORE.

___ Check here when you've completed today's dare.

How did you choose to show honor? What was the result?
What are some other ways you could demonstrate honor in the
coming days?

_____

_____

_____

_____

_____

_____

_____

I will also honor them and they will not be insignificant. (Jeremiah 30:19)

"The Love Dare will change your life. Be prepared
and don't quit. Love your wife like God loves you."—Dale

DAY 16
Love intercedes

*Beloved, I pray that in all respects you may prosper and
be in good health, just as your soul prospers.* —3 John 2

You cannot change your spouse. As much as you may
want to, you cannot play God and reach into their heart and
mold them into what you want them to be. But that's what
most couples spend a large part of their time trying to do—
change their spouse.

Insanity has been described as doing the same thing over
and over but expecting different results. But isn't that what happens when you try to change your mate? It's frustration at the
highest level. At some point you have to accept that it's not
something you can do. But here's what you *can* do. You can
become a "wise farmer."

A farmer cannot make a seed grow into a fruitful crop. He
cannot argue, manipulate, or demand it to bear fruit. But he
can plant the seed into fertile soil, give it water and nutrients,
protect it from weeds, and then turn it over to God. Millions
of farmers have made a livelihood from this process over the
centuries. They know that not every seed sprouts. But most *will*
grow when planted in proper soil and given what they need.

There is no guarantee that anything in this book will
change your spouse. But that's not what this book is about.
It's about you daring to love. And if you take the Love Dare
seriously, there is a high likelihood that you will be personally
changed from the inside out.

If you carry out each dare, your spouse will likely be
affected and your marriage will hopefully begin to bloom in

front of your eyes. It may take weeks. It may even take years. But regardless of the soil you're working with, you are to plan for success. You are to get the weeds out of your marriage. You are to nurture the soil of your mate's heart and then depend on God for the results.

But you won't be able to do this alone. You will need something that is more powerful than anything else you have. And that "something" is effective prayer.

Prayer really does work. It's a spiritual phenomenon created by an unlimited, powerful God. And it yields amazing results.

Do you feel like giving up on your marriage? Jesus said to pray instead of quitting (Luke 18:1). Are you stressed out and worried? Prayer can bring peace to your storms (Philippians 4:6–7). Do you need a major breakthrough? Prayer can make the difference (Acts 12:1–17).

God is sovereign. He does things His way. He's not a genie in a lamp that submits to your every wish. But He does love you and desires an intimate relationship with you. And a thriving walk with Him doesn't happen apart from prayer.

There are some key elements that must be in place for prayer to be effective. But suffice it to say that prayer works best when coming from a humble heart that is in a right relationship with God and others. The Bible says, "Confess your sins to one another, and pray for one another. . . . The effective prayer of a righteous man can accomplish much" (James 5:16).

Have you ever wondered why God gives you overwhelming insight into your spouse's hidden faults? Do you really think it's for endless nagging? No, it is for effective kneeling. No one knows better how to pray for your mate than you.

Has your scolding or nagging been working? The answer is no, because that's not what changes a heart. It is time to try talking to God in your prayer closet instead.

A husband will find that God can "fix" his wife a lot better than *he* can. A wife will accomplish more through strategic prayer than from all her persuasive efforts. It is also a much more pleasant way to live.

So turn your complaints into prayers and watch the Master work while you keep your hands clean. If your spouse doesn't have any type of relationship with God, then it's clear what you need to start praying for.

Beyond this, begin to pray for exactly what your mate needs. Pray for his heart. Pray for her attitude. Pray for your spouse's responsibilities before God. Pray for truth to replace lies. Pray that forgiveness would replace bitterness. Pray for a genuine breakthrough in your marriage. And then pray for your heart's desires—for love and honor to become the norm. Pray for romance and intimacy to go to a deeper level.

One of the most loving things you can ever do for your spouse is to pray for them. "Ask, and it will be given to you; seek, and you will find; knock, and it will be opened to you" (Matthew 7:7).

TODAY'S DARE

BEGIN PRAYING TODAY FOR YOUR SPOUSE'S
HEART. PRAY FOR THREE SPECIFIC AREAS
WHERE YOU DESIRE FOR GOD TO WORK IN
YOUR SPOUSE'S LIFE AND IN YOUR MARRIAGE.

___ Check here when you've completed today's dare.

Have you experienced the power of prayer in the past?
What did you choose to pray about? Was it easy for you, or did
it feel foreign to you?

_____

_____

_____

_____

_____

_____

_____

_____

_____

_____

_____

*For insight into how to pray more effectively, as well as ideas on praying
for your spouse, see the Appendix, pages 210 and 214.*

If anyone is God-fearing and does His will, He listens to him. (John 9:31)

DAY 17
Love promotes intimacy

He who covers over an offense promotes love, but whoever repeats the matter separates close friends. —Proverbs 17:9 NIV

Who are you the closest to in life? With whom do you share your secrets? It may be a good friend you've known since childhood or college. It may be a sibling, parent, or coworker. But nothing rivals the closeness that can be experienced between a husband and wife. Marriage is designed to be the most intimate of all human relationships—emotionally, physically, and spiritually.

That's why it is so beautiful and why we need it so much. We long for a best friend with whom we can share our hearts. A safe, loyal companion who *gets* us, understanding who we are. Someone who knows our deepest secrets and yet still accepts us in spite of them. Intimacy is described as being "fully known and fully loved."

But sadly, many marriages lack the intimacy that God desires between a man and his wife. For this great blessing is also the site of its greatest danger. Someone who knows us this intimately can either love us at depths we never imagined, or can wound us in ways we may never recover from. This is both the fire and fear of marriage. It's why creating a very safe place for one another to open up is fundamental for intimacy to thrive.

What are you experiencing the most in your home right now? Are you open books, or more like closed vaults? How much do you two really talk? How much do you trust each other with your secrets? Would your mate say you make them feel safe, or scared? Especially if you've wounded one another in the past, you will tend to be guarded and hide from intimacy.

If home is not considered a place of emotional safety, you will both be tempted to seek it somewhere else. Perhaps you might look to another person, initiating a relationship that either flirts with adultery or actually enters in. You may look for a safe escape in work or in outside hobbies, something that shields you from intimacy.

But regardless of your situation, love can help you rediscover intimacy with your spouse. "There is no fear in love; but perfect love casts out fear" (1 John 4:18). Your mate should not feel pressured to be perfect in order to receive your attention and approval. He or she should not walk on eggshells in the very place where they ought to feel the most comfortable in their bare feet. The atmosphere in your marriage should be one of freedom. Like Adam and Eve in the garden, your coexistence at home should only intensify your intimacy. Being "naked" and "not ashamed" (Genesis 2:25) should always be in the same sentence, right in your marriage—physically and emotionally.

Admittedly, this is tender territory. Marriage has unloaded another person's sinfulness and baggage into your life, and yours into theirs. Both of you may feel misunderstood and unloved, which is the opposite of intimacy. But today begins an opportunity to wrap your mate's private information in the protective embrace of your love, and recommit to being the one who can best help him or her deal with it.

Some secrets may need correcting. Therefore, you can be an agent of compassion and healing—not by lecturing or criticizing, but by listening in love and then gently speaking truth when they feel safe enough to receive it from you.

Some secrets just need accepting. They are part of this person's makeup and history. And though unpleasant, these issues always require a gentle touch. In either case, you alone wield the power either to reject your spouse because of what you know or to welcome them in—warts and all. They will either know they're in a refuge of safety where they are free to make mistakes, or they will recoil into themselves and be lost to you, perhaps forever. Loving them well should be your life's work.

Consider it this way. No one knows you more intimately than God, the One who made you. The writer of Psalm 139 was right when he prayed, "You know when I sit down and when I rise up; You understand my thought from afar. You scrutinize my path and my lying down, and are intimately acquainted with all my ways. Even before there is a word on my tongue, behold, O Lord, You know it all" (Psalm 139:2–4).

And yet God, who knows every secret about us, loves us at a depth we cannot begin to fathom (Ephesians 3:19). How much more should we—as imperfect people—reach out to our spouse in grace, accepting them for who they are and assuring them their friendship and secrets are safe with us?

This may be an area where you've failed in the past. If so, don't expect your mate to immediately give you wide-open access to their heart. You must begin to rebuild trust slowly. To stop avoiding them and start talking. To listen compassionately, accept them more genuinely, and then love them more deeply.

Jesus Himself is described as One who doesn't barge into people's lives but who stands at the door and knocks. He said, "If anyone hears My voice and opens the door, I will come in to him and will dine with him, and he with Me" (Revelation 3:20).

The reality of intimacy always takes time to develop, especially after being compromised. But it is worth the endless treasures found beneath its guarded lock. Your loving commitment to reestablishing it may be the key to opening it—for anyone willing to take the dare.

TODAY'S DARE

BEGIN BUILDING EMOTIONAL INTIMACY
WITH YOUR MATE. DETERMINE TODAY TO
GUARD YOUR MATE'S SECRETS (UNLESS THEY
ARE DANGEROUS TO THEM OR TO YOU) AND TO
PRAY FOR THEM. TALK WITH YOUR SPOUSE AND
LISTEN WITH ACCEPTANCE, OPENING UP TO
THEM AS WELL. MAKE THEM FEEL SAFE.

___ Check here when you've completed today's dare.

Given that the safer people feel, the more they open up,
what does this say about your marriage in the past? How hard
is it for you to listen and hold back from saying something,
critical or otherwise? What have you learned about your
spouse today, simply from listening?

I am my beloved's and my beloved is mine. (Song of Solomon 6:3)

"You have to believe in this and not give up hope. I haven't."—*Francisco*

DAY 18
Love seeks to understand

How blessed is the man who finds wisdom,
and the man who gains understanding. —*Proverbs 3:13*

We enjoy discovering as much as we can about the things we truly care about. If it's our favorite football team, we'll read any article that helps us keep up with how they're doing. If it's cooking, we'll check out those channels or Web sites that share the best grilling techniques or dessert recipes. If there's a subject that appeals to us, we'll take notice any time it comes up. In fact, it naturally becomes our area of personal study.

It's fine, of course, to have various interests and become knowledgeable about specific areas of preference. But this is where love would ask the question, "How much do you know about your mate?"

Think back to the days when you were courting. Didn't you study the one your heart was yearning for?

When a man is trying to win the heart of a woman, he studies her. He learns her likes, dislikes, habits, and hobbies. But after he wins her heart and marries her, he often stops learning about her. The mystery and challenge of knowing her seems less intriguing, and he finds his interests drifting to other areas.

This is also true in many cases for women, who start off admiring and building respect for the man they desire to be with. But after marriage, those feelings begin to fade as reality reveals that her "prince" is a flawed and imperfect man.

Yet there are many good things still to be discovered about your spouse. And this understanding will help draw you closer together. It can even give you favor in the eyes of your mate. "Good understanding produces favor" (Proverbs 13:15).

Consider the following perspective: if the amount you studied your spouse before marriage were equal to a high school diploma, then you should continue to learn about your mate until you gain a "college degree," a "master's degree," and ultimately a "doctorate degree." Think of it as a lifelong journey that draws your heart ever closer to your mate.

- Do you know his or her greatest hopes and dreams?
- Do you fully understand how they prefer to give and receive love?
- Do you know what your spouse's greatest fears are and why they struggle with them?

Some of the problems you have in relating to your spouse are simply because you don't understand them. They probably react very differently to certain situations than you do, and you can't figure out why. These differences—even the ones that are relatively insignificant—can be the cause of many fights and conflicts in your marriage. That's because, as the Bible says, we tend to "revile" those things we don't understand (Jude 10).

There are reasons for his or her tastes and preferences. Each nuance in your spouse's character has a back story. Each element of who he is, how he thinks, and what he's like is couched in a set of guiding principles, which often makes sense only to the person who holds them. But it's worth the time it will take to study *why* they are the *way* they are.

If you miss the level of intimacy you once shared with your spouse, one of the best ways to unlock their heart again is by making a commitment to know them. Study them. Read them like a book you're trying to understand. A treasure chest to be unlocked.

Ask questions. The Bible says, "The ear of the wise seeks knowledge" (Proverbs 18:15). Love takes the initiative to begin conversations. In order to get your mate to open up, they need to know that your desire for understanding them is real and genuine.

Listen. "A fool does not delight in understanding, but only in revealing his own mind" (Proverbs 18:2). The goal of understanding your mate is to hear them, not merely to tell them what you think. Even if your spouse is not very talkative, love calls you to draw out the "deep water" that dwells within them (Proverbs 20:5).

Ask God for discernment. "The Lord gives wisdom; from His mouth come knowledge and understanding" (Proverbs 2:6). Things like gender differences, family backgrounds, and varied life experiences can cloud your ability to know your mate's heart and motivations. But God is a giver of wisdom. He can show you what you need in order to know how to love your spouse better.

"By wisdom a house is built, and by understanding it is established; and by knowledge the rooms are filled with all precious and pleasant riches" (Proverbs 24:3–4). There is a depth of beauty and meaning inside your wife or husband that will amaze you as you discover more of it. Enter the mystery with expectation and enthusiasm. Desire to know this person even better than you do now. Make him or her your chosen field of study, and you will fill your home with the kind of riches only love can provide.

TODAY'S DARE

PREPARE A SPECIAL DINNER AT HOME, JUST FOR THE TWO OF YOU. THE DINNER CAN BE AS NICE AS YOU PREFER. FOCUS THIS TIME ON GETTING TO KNOW YOUR SPOUSE BETTER, PERHAPS IN AREAS YOU'VE RARELY TALKED ABOUT. DETERMINE TO MAKE IT AN ENJOYABLE EVENING FOR YOU AND YOUR MATE.

___ Check here when you've completed today's dare.

What did you learn about your spouse that you didn't know before? How could you continue this process of discovery in other ways, at other times? What were some of the moments that made this evening memorable?

For a list of questions related to today's dare, see the Appendix, page 206.

Acquire wisdom; and with all your acquiring, get understanding. (Proverbs 4:7)

DAY 19
Love is impossible

Let us love one another, for love is from God; and everyone
who loves is born of God and knows God. —1 John 4:7

The Love Dare starts with a secret. And though it's been an
unspoken element throughout each day, you've likely grown
more and more aware of it all the time. The secret is this: you
cannot manufacture unconditional love (*agape* love) out of your
own imperfect heart. It's impossible. It's beyond your natural
ability. It's beyond all of our capabilities.

You may not want to believe that. You may be convinced
that with enough hard work and commitment, you can muster
up unstoppable, lifelong, and sacrificial love from within.
And while, yes, you may be able to demonstrate kindness and
patience at times, and while you may have learned to be more
thoughtful and considerate than before, the task of sincerely
and consistently loving someone unselfishly and unconditionally is another matter altogether.

How many times, for example, has your love failed to keep
you from deceiving or manipulating, from lusting or envying,
from overreacting or exaggerating, or from thinking judgmental or unkind thoughts? How many times has your love proven
incapable of controlling your anger? How many times has your
love failed to motivate you to willingly apologize, fully forgive,
or bring about a peaceable end to an ongoing argument?

It's this failure that exposes mankind's sinful condition.
Our *own* sinful condition. We've all fallen short of God's standards and commands (Romans 3:23). We've all demonstrated
selfishness, hatred, and pride. And unless something is done

to cleanse us of these ungodlike attributes, we will all stand before God displeasing to Him (Psalm 5:4), guilty as charged (Romans 6:23). That's why if you're not in a right relationship with God, you cannot truly love your spouse, because He is the Source of that love.

You can't give what you don't have. You can't call up reserves that aren't already there. Selfish springs do not produce selfless water. Just as you can't give away a million dollars that you don't have, you cannot pay out love in greater measure than you own. You can try, but you will fail.

Love that is faithfully pure and able to withstand every pressure is out of your reach, as long as you're only looking within yourself to find it. You need another source. You need someone to give you that kind of love. But here's the good news: because of God's great love for you and His love for your spouse, He has made a way to express His love *through* you.

"Love is from God" (1 John 4:7). The Scriptures consistently communicate that the way we discover love is by turning to God's Son, Jesus Christ, who was sent to earth to be both the example and source of perfect love. It is only when we turn away from our selfishness and sincerely ask Jesus to step into our lives and take control of us that our deepest need for love is met and our greatest ability to love begins. Like a branch disconnected from the vine, Jesus said, "Apart from Me, you can do nothing" (John 15:5). This includes loving your spouse unconditionally.

But "if you abide in Me," He went on to say, "and My words abide in you, ask whatever you wish, and it will be done for you" (John 15:7). That word "abide" means to stay relationally close. This is not religious jargon but a spiritual invitation. By entering into a daily relationship with Jesus, you can "know the love of Christ which passes knowledge; that you may be filled with all the fullness of God" (Ephesians 3:19 NKJV). You can then love. Unconditionally.

By surrendering yourself to Christ, His power can work through you. He "is able to do far more abundantly beyond all that we ask or think, according to the power that works within us" (Ephesians 3:20). That's how you love your spouse.

So your inadequacy and inability—as defeating as they may feel—have a happy ending if you will reach out in faith and receive the love God has for you. Then the love He has "poured out within our hearts through the Holy Spirit who was given to us" (Romans 5:5) will always be available to you, every time you admit your inadequacy and trust in His ability.

You simply won't be able to do it without Him. But people are constantly discovering that they can . . . *with* Him.

Perhaps you've never given your heart to Christ, but you sense Him drawing you today. You may be realizing for the first time that you, too, have broken God's commands, and that your guilt will keep you from knowing Him. But Scripture says that if you repent by turning away from your sin and turning to God, He is willing to forgive you because of the sacrifice His Son made through His death on the cross. He is pursuing you, not to enslave you but to free you, so you can receive His love and forgiveness. Then you can share it with the one you've been called most specifically to love.

Perhaps you're already a believer, but you would admit that you have walked away from fellowship with God. You're not in the Word, you're not in prayer, maybe you're not even in church anymore. The love you used to feel coursing through your veins has dwindled into apathy.

The truth is, you cannot *live* without Him and you cannot *love* without Him. But there is no telling what He could do in your marriage if you choose to put your trust in Him.

LOOK BACK OVER THE DARES FROM PREVIOUS
DAYS. DO THEY REVEAL A DIFFICULTY IN YOUR
ABILITY TO LOVE YOUR SPOUSE? DID SOME
SEEM IMPOSSIBLE? HAVE YOU REALIZED YOUR
NEED FOR GOD TO CHANGE YOUR HEART AND
GIVE YOU HIS ABILITY TO LOVE? ASK HIM TO
SHOW YOU WHERE YOU STAND WITH HIM AND
TO GIVE YOU THE GRACE TO SEEK HIM,
FIND HIM, AND WALK WITH HIM.

___ Check here when you've completed today's dare.

What do you believe God is saying to you? Is there a stir-
ring in your heart? What decision have you made in response
to this?

_____

_____

_____

_____

_____

_____

_____

This is impossible, but with God all things are possible. (Matthew 19:26)

_____

_____

_____

_____

_____

_____

_____

_____

_____

_____

_____

_____

_____

_____

_____

_____

_____

_____

_____

_____

_____

_____

_____

"I realized that the Love Dare journey is really about me
forming my relationship with God."—Connie

DAY 20
Love is Jesus Christ

While we were still helpless, at the right time
Christ died for the ungodly. —Romans 5:6

Do you feel loved by God? You should. Deeply. You will never fully love others until you first grasp His love for you personally. "The one who does not love does not know God, for God is love" (1 John 4:8).

God not only loved you in how He created you and has provided every breath and sustained your life, but He loved you the most through the gift of His Son. The most famous verse in the Bible says this: "For God so loved the world, that He gave His only begotten Son, that whoever believes in Him shall not perish, but have eternal life" (John 3:16).

For centuries, millions of people around the world have found God's love and a relationship with Him through these truths—truths that summarize God's great love for you personally and His greatest offer to you now. Jesus has come "to seek and to save" you (Luke 19:10). But from what?

The Bible explains we are each born in a selfish state that is bent toward sin (Psalm 51:5). Then we, by our own choosing, become prideful, deceitful, hateful, lustful, resistant to authority, and ungrateful—neither fearing God or knowing God (Romans 3:9–20). "All of us have become like one who is unclean, and all our righteous deeds are like a filthy garment" (Isaiah 64:6).

But God looked down on the earth and saw mankind in our ignorance and dirty condition (Psalm 14:2–3). He knew that without His intervention, we would have no hope of purifying ourselves or becoming good enough to walk with Him or spend an eternity with Him in heaven.

He also knew that His justice would require judgment upon our sin (Romans 6:23). It's not as though God sends innocent people to hell. We stand guilty. We deserve it. Every last one of us (Ephesians 2:1–7).

However, in His love and mercy, "God has sent His only begotten Son into the world so that we might live through Him" (1 John 4:9). Jesus Christ "bore our sins in His body on the cross, so that we might die to sin and live to righteousness" (1 Peter 2:24). By His death, Jesus forever made invalid the very idea that you are not loved. If you ever feel unloved, you're not looking at the cross. He proved His love for you there.

Love this deep cannot be fully understood. "One will hardly die for a righteous man; though perhaps for the good man someone would dare even to die. But God demonstrates His own love toward us, in that *while we were yet sinners,* Christ died for us" (Romans 5:7–8).

Nor can love like this be earned. "For by grace you have been saved through faith; and that not of yourselves, it is the gift of God; not as a result of works, so that no one may boast" (Ephesians 2:8–9).

But it must be received. "If you confess with your mouth Jesus as Lord, and believe in your heart that God raised Him from the dead, you will be saved" (Romans 10:9).

And when you have received this new life and love as your own, you are enabled to love in ways you've never been capable of loving before.

"This is how we know what love is: Jesus Christ laid down his life for us. And we ought to lay down our lives for our brothers. . . . This is his command: to believe in the name of his

Son, Jesus Christ, and to love one another as he commanded us" (1 John 3:16, 23 NIV).

Every failure in your life, all the good you haven't been able to do, every minute you've wasted—all of it can be forgiven and made right by putting your life into the hands of the One who first gave His love and life for you.

Maybe you've never done this. Then today is your day. "Now is the acceptable time, behold, now is the day of salvation" (2 Corinthians 6:2).

Maybe you did it years ago, but you've wandered far from your spiritual roots. Then "repent and return, so that your sins may be wiped away, in order that times of refreshing may come from the presence of the Lord" (Acts 3:19).

He was willing to love you even though you didn't deserve it, even when you didn't love back. He saw all your flaws and still chose to love you. His love made the greatest sacrifice to meet your greatest need. As a result, you are able (by His grace) to walk in the fullness and blessing of His love.

Now and forever.

And then you can experience and share this same love with your spouse. You can love even when you're not loved in return. You can see all their flaws and imperfections and still choose to love. And you can become His instrument, one of the most personal ways He meets the needs of your spouse. As a result, they can walk in the fullness and blessing of your love. Now and till death.

True love is found in Jesus Christ. And after you have received His loving gift of new life, His sacrificial death in your place, and His forgiveness for your sins, then you are finally ready to live the dare.

TODAY'S DARE

DARE TO TRUST WHAT GOD IS SAYING
TO YOU THROUGH HIS WORD. DARE TO TRUST
JESUS CHRIST FOR YOUR SALVATION. DARE
TO PRAY, "LORD JESUS, I'M A SINNER. BUT YOU
HAVE SHOWN YOUR LOVE FOR ME BY DYING
TO FORGIVE MY SINS, AND YOU HAVE PROVEN
YOUR POWER TO SAVE ME FROM DEATH BY
YOUR RESURRECTION. LORD, CHANGE MY
HEART, AND SAVE ME BY YOUR GRACE.
FILL ME WITH YOUR LOVE."

___ Check here when you've completed today's dare.

Write about what this experience has been like for you.
Even if you are only renewing your commitment to receive
and express His love, what has He shown you today?

To learn more about the salvation Christ offers you, see the Appendix, page 216.

In His love and in His mercy He redeemed them. (Isaiah 63:9)

DAY 21
Love is satisfied in God

The Lord will continually guide you, and satisfy your desire.
—Isaiah 58:11

Day 20 was a vitally important day in the Love Dare—and hopefully in your life—as we discussed the glaring need of every human heart. You may have already known or just come to realize that nothing in your toolbox of talents and resources could wash away the stains or repair the damage that sin has left behind, and that Jesus is the One sent by God to supply what you've been missing. If you've received Him by faith and have turned your life over to Him to lead, then His Holy Spirit—this very moment—is renewing and filling your heart. His grace and power can now be released into everything you do. Including, not the least, your own marriage.

But whether this is new territory for you, or you've long been a follower of Jesus, now is the time to firm up one thing in your mind: you need God *every single day*. Because He alone can satisfy. Walking with Him is not a part-time proposition.

Too often people think money, fame, accomplishment, or power will make them happy. King Solomon attained all of these things in great measure and repeatedly discovered that "all was vanity and striving after wind" (Ecclesiastes 2:1–25). He concluded that since all good things come from God's hand, "who can have enjoyment without Him?" (verse 25).

And yet whenever we feel low on happiness, we often think it's because of something we want but don't have. We don't realize that God did not create things on earth that can satisfy us more than He does—even our spouses. He formed the longings within us so that we would seek Him and be filled with His heavenly supply. True and lasting love, joy, and peace are found only in Him (Galatians 5:22).

Your husband may be late coming home. Again.

But God will always be right on time.

Your wife may have let you down. Again.

But God can always be trusted to deliver on His promises.

Every day you place expectations on your spouse. Sometimes they meet them; sometimes they don't. But never will they be able to satisfy totally all the demands you ask of them—partly because some of your demands are unreasonable, and partly because your mate is only human.

God, however, is not. And those who approach Him in utter dependence each day for the real needs in their lives are the ones who find out just how dependable He is.

Can your spouse give you inner peace? No. But God can. "Be anxious for nothing, but in everything by prayer and supplication with thanksgiving let your requests be made known to God. And the peace of God, which surpasses all comprehension, will guard your hearts and your minds in Christ Jesus" (Philippians 4:6–7).

Can your spouse enable you to be content no matter what life throws at you? No. But God can. "I have learned to be content in whatever circumstances I am," the apostle Paul said. "In any and every circumstance I have learned the secret of being filled. . . . I can do all things through Him who strengthens me" (Philippians 4:11–13).

So stop expecting someone or something to keep you functioning and fulfilled on a nonstop basis. It's not fun for you or fair to them. Only God can "supply all your needs according to His riches in glory in Christ Jesus" as you learn to depend on Him (Philippians 4:19).

Your needs for love, intimacy, acceptance, peace, joy, and adequacy are real. No one is saying you shouldn't have them. But rather than trying to fill them by plugging into things that are unstable at best and are subject to change—your health, your money, even the affections and best intentions of your mate—plug into God instead. He's the only One in your life who never changes. His faithfulness, truth, and promises to His children will always remain.

That's why you need to seek Him every day.

When you pursue happiness through earthly things, you end up missing God and not being happy either. But when you lose yourself in the pursuit of loving and pleasing Him, you not only get an intimate relationship with God, but He also gives you happiness as gravy on the side. The Bible says, "Delight yourself in the Lord; and He will give you the desires of your heart" (Psalm 37:4). When you are seeking Him first, loving Him first, making your relationship with Him top priority, He promises to supply you with what you really need—which, actually, is all it really takes to satisfy you.

Jesus once spoke to a woman at a Samaritan well who had tried getting her needs met through five different failed marriages. But standing there before Him with both her life and her water bucket empty, she found in Christ what He called "living water" (John 4:10)—a supply that wasn't just for quenching temporary thirst. He offered her a drink of soul satisfaction that never quits giving and refreshing. And this is what's available to you at each sunrise and each night before bed, no matter who your spouse is or what they've done to you.

"In Your presence is fullness of joy," King David wrote to God. "In Your right hand there are pleasures forever" (Psalm 16:11). God is your everyday supply . . . of everything you need.

TODAY'S DARE

BE INTENTIONAL TODAY ABOUT MAKING
A TIME TO PRAY AND READ YOUR BIBLE.
TRY READING A CHAPTER OUT OF PSALMS OR
PROVERBS EACH DAY, OR READING A CHAPTER
IN THE GOSPEL BOOK OF JOHN. AS YOU DO,
IMMERSE YOURSELF IN GOD'S LOVE AND FIND
REST IN THE PROMISES AND PEACE HE
HAS FOR YOU. THIS WILL ADD TO YOUR
GROWTH AS YOU WALK WITH HIM.

___ Check here when you've completed today's dare.

How do you think spending time daily with God will change your situation and perspective? How can you make Him a bigger part of your day?

You open Your hand and satisfy the desire of every living thing. (Psalm 145:16)

"I really believe that God can make it possible to work through
any situation. The Love Dare is proving my belief."—Samantha

DAY 22
Love is faithful

I will betroth you to Me in faithfulness.
Then you will know the Lord. —Hosea 2:20

As Christians, love is the basis of our whole identity. As God's children, He gives us the name "Beloved," which means we are *ones who are unconditionally loved by God*. The focus of our lives becomes loving God and loving others.

Jesus clarified God's greatest command for us by saying, "You shall love the Lord your God with all your heart . . . your soul . . . your strength . . . your mind . . . and your neighbor as yourself" (Luke 10:27).

Our love for each other is supposed to be how people distinguish us as Christ's disciples (John 13:35). It is the root and ground of our existence (Ephesians 3:17), meant to be expressed with passion and fervency (1 Peter 4:8). Love is an exercise we are to "abound" in more and more (1 Thessalonians 3:12), always getting better at it, becoming increasingly defined by it.

So if love is what we were created to share, what do you do when your love is rejected? How do you handle it when the one to whom you've pledged your life stops accepting the love you're called to give?

The account of the prophet Hosea is one of the most remarkable in the Bible. Against all logic and propriety, God instructed him to marry a prostitute. He wanted Hosea's marriage to show what heaven's unconditional love looks like toward us. Hosea's union with Gomer produced three children but, as expected, this woman who had long made her living in immorality was not content to stay faithful to one man. So Hosea was left to deal with a broken heart and the shame of abandonment.

He had loved her, but she had spurned his love. They had grown close, but now she had been disloyal and adulterous, rejecting him for the lust of total strangers.

Time passed, and God spoke to Hosea again, telling him to go and reaffirm his love for this woman who had been repeatedly unfaithful. By now, however, she had reached a new low and was being sold as a dirty, unwanted slave. But Hosea paid the price for her redemption and brought her home. Yes, she had treated his love with contempt. She had dealt treacherously with his heart. Yet he welcomed her back into his life, expressing an unconditional love toward her.

This is a true story, but God used it to paint a lasting picture of His love for us. Through Hosea's actions we see a God who showers His favor on us without measure, though we often don't pay attention in return. At times we have acted shamefully and deemed His love an intrusion, as if it is keeping us from what we really want. We have rejected Him in many ways—even after receiving His gift of eternal salvation—and yet He still loves us. He still remains faithful.

Even so, His love doesn't keep Him from calling us to account for our mistreatment of Him. We pay more of a price for our rejection than we often realize. Yet He still chooses to respond with grace and mercy. "In Him we have redemption through His blood, the forgiveness of our trespasses, according to the riches of His grace" (Ephesians 1:7). In Him we have the model of what rejected love does. It stays faithful.

Jesus called His followers to this kind of love in the passage known as the Sermon on the Mount. He said to "love your enemies, do good to those who hate you, bless those who curse you, pray for those who mistreat you" (Luke 6:27–28). After all, "If you love those who love you, what credit is that to you? For even sinners love those who love them. If you do good to those who do good to you, what credit is that to you? For even sinners do the same" (Luke 6:32–33).

He said, "Love your enemies, and do good, and lend, expecting nothing in return; and your reward will be great, and you will be sons of the Most High; for He Himself is kind to ungrateful and evil men" (Luke 6:35).

From the vantage point of the wedding altar, you would never have dreamed that the person you married might later become to you a kind of "enemy," one you would need to love as a difficult and even painful sacrifice. And yet far too often in marriage, the relationship does indeed dwindle down to that level. Even to the point of betrayal or, sadly, to unfaithfulness.

For many, this is the beginning of the end. Some respond by rapidly moving toward a tragic divorce. Others, more protective of their reputation in the eyes of others, decide to keep the charade going. But they have no intention of liking it or trying any harder—much less of truly loving again.

This is not the model, however, for the follower of Christ. If love is to be like His, it must love even when its overtures are returned unwanted. And for your love to be like that, it must be His love to begin with.

The reason why you still have hope of giving undeserved love to your spouse is because God has given His undeserved love to you—repeatedly, enduringly. Love is often expressed the most to those who deserve it the least.

Ask Him to fill you with the kind of love only He can provide, then purpose to give it to your mate in a way that reflects your gratefulness to God for loving you. That's the beauty of redeeming love. That's the power of faithfulness.

TODAY'S DARE

LOVE IS A CHOICE, NOT A FEELING. IT IS
AN INITIATED ACTION, NOT AN IMPULSIVE
REACTION. CHOOSE TODAY TO BE COMMITTED
TO LOVE EVEN IF YOUR SPOUSE HAS LOST MOST
OF THEIR INTEREST IN RECEIVING IT. SAY TO
THEM TODAY, IN WORDS SIMILAR TO THESE,
"I LOVE YOU. PERIOD. AND NO MATTER WHAT
YOU DO, I WILL NEVER STOP LOVING YOU."

___ Check here when you've completed today's dare.

Why is this kind of love impossible without the love of
Christ beating in your heart? How does His presence within
you enable you to love, even when it's primarily one-sided?

_____

_____

_____

_____

_____

_____

_____

I have chosen the faithful way. (Psalm 119:30)

"It's been three weeks, and she is starting to notice a difference."—Bob

Day 23
Love always protects

[Love] always protects. —*1 Corinthians 13:7* NIV

No couple gets married as enemies. They tie the knot filled with hopes of a lifetime of love. But the high rate of divorce reveals that after a couple walks down the aisle, they are stepping into a minefield of marital obstacles that can take either of them down. Sadly, every marriage has enemies out there.

That's why love compels us to be on the alert and guard what is most dear and precious to us, to be willing to step up and fight some battles passionately—those that pertain to protecting our spouse and the strength of our union. Many things could destroy our relationship unless our love puts on armor and picks up a sword to protect its own.

Here, for example, are just a few of the potential attacks you need to be aware of and engaged in, constantly protecting your mate and your marriage. Responsibility, not passivity, is the key to guarding against the following issues . . .

Misplaced priorities. Any good thing has the potential to become a harmful thing if it becomes an all-consuming thing. Friends, hobbies, and work schedules must be kept in balance and in their proper place. You can't protect your home when you're rarely there, nor when you're relationally disconnected. Even your children, while obviously a key priority, should be raised on the foundation of your strong marriage. When parents invert this and prioritize the kids above their marriage, they actually hurt their children in the long run as the marriage is weakened. One of the most commonly heard excuses for divorce is that it's "best for the children." But what's best for the

children is seeing their mom and dad demonstrate unconditional love for each other, keep their commitments, work out
their differences, forgive and preserve a legacy of endurance.

Unhealthy relationships. Not everyone has the material to
be a good friend. Not every man you hunt and fish with speaks
wisely when it comes to matters of marriage. Not every woman
in your lunch group has a perfect perspective on commitment
and priorities. In fact, anyone who undermines your marriage
does not deserve the right to whisper in your ear.

Harmful influences. Are you allowing certain habits to poison
your home? Technology, television, and the Internet can be productive and enjoyable additions to your life, but they can also
invite destructive content into your home and drain away precious, countless hours from your family. Be careful and cautious
of anything that could deaden your mind or steal your time.

Sexual temptation. Be on guard at all times from allowing opposite-sex relationships—at work, at the gym, even at
church—to draw you emotionally away from the one to whom
you've already given your heart. Many divorces are now resulting from unguarded use of social networking sites. Staring at
smiling pictures of old friends and old flames can hook you
emotionally and deceptively lure your heart away from the
love of your life and into a danger zone. Any relationship that
is drawing your affection away from your spouse has already
gone too far. Wisdom says to be extra guarded around those
you find most appealing and attractive. They should be kept at
a greater emotional distance. Why? Your love is why.

Shame. Everyone deals with some level of inferiority and
weakness. And because marriage has a way of exposing it all to
you and your mate, you need to protect your wife or husband's
vulnerability by never speaking negatively about them in
public. Their secrets are your secrets (unless, of course, these

involve destructive behaviors that are putting you, your children, or themselves in grave danger). Generally speaking, love hides the fault of others. It covers their shame.

Parasites. Watch out for parasites. A parasite is anything that latches onto you or your partner and sucks the life out of your marriage. They're usually in the form of addictions, like gambling, drugs, or pornography. They promise pleasure but grow like a disease and consume more and more of your thoughts, time, and money. They steal away your loyalty and heart from those you love. Marriages rarely survive if parasites are present. If you love your spouse, you must destroy any addiction that has your heart. If you don't, it will destroy you.

So as a wife, realize you have a role as protector in your marriage. You must guard your heart from being led away through any novels, magazines, and other forms of entertainment that blur your perception of reality and put unfair expectations on your husband. Do your part in helping him feel strong, while avoiding talk-show thinking that lures your attention away from your family. "The wise woman builds her house, but the foolish tears it down with her own hands" (Proverbs 14:1).

And husbands, you are the head of your home. You are the one responsible before God for guarding the gate and standing your ground against anything that would threaten your wife or marriage. This is no small assignment. It requires a heart of courage and a head for preemptive action. Jesus said, "If the head of the house had known at what time of the night the thief was coming, he would have been on the alert and would not have allowed his house to be broken into" (Matthew 24:43). This role is yours. Take it seriously.

TODAY'S DARE

REMOVE ANYTHING THAT IS HINDERING
YOUR RELATIONSHIP, ANY ADDICTION OR
INFLUENCE THAT IS STEALING YOUR
AFFECTIONS AND TURNING YOUR HEART
AWAY FROM YOUR SPOUSE.

___ Check here when you've completed today's dare.

What did you throw out first? Are there others that need to go as well? What do you hope the removal of these things will do for you, your marriage, and your relationship with God?

For help in dealing with the "parasite" of pornography, see the Appendix, page 220.

You will be restored if you remove unrighteousness far from your tent. (Job 22:23)

DAY 24
Love vs. Lust

The world is passing away, and also its lusts;
but the one who does the will of God lives forever. —1 John 2:17

Adam and Eve were supplied with everything they needed in the garden of Eden. They had fellowship with God and intimacy with one another. But after Eve was deceived by the serpent, she saw the forbidden fruit and set her heart on it. Then Adam joined her in sin, and they both ate against God's command.

That's the progression. From eyes to heart to action. And then follow shame and regret.

We, too, have been supplied by God with everything we need for a full, productive, enriching life. Jesus promised that our material needs for food and clothing would always be provided to God's children (Matthew 6:25–33), and the Bible goes on to say that we should be "content" with these (1 Timothy 6:8). God's blessings, however, go so far beyond fundamental needs. He richly lavishes His love, Spirit, and Word upon us.

Yet like Adam and Eve, we still want more. So we set our eyes and hearts on seeking worldly pleasure. We try to meet legitimate needs in illegitimate ways. For many it's seeking sexual fulfillment in another person or in pornographic images designed to feel like a real person. We look, stare, and fantasize. We try to be discreet but barely turn our eyes away. And once our eyes are captured by curiosity, our hearts become entangled. Then we act on our lust.

We can also lust after money, possessions, power, or prideful ambition. We see what others have and we want it. Our hearts are deceived into saying, "I could be happy if I only had this." Then we make the decision to go after it. "But those who want to get rich fall into temptation and a snare and many foolish and harmful desires which plunge men into ruin and destruction" (1 Timothy 6:9).

Lust is in opposition to love. Instead of being grateful for what God has given us, we set our hearts on something outside the boundaries of His provision. Lust makes good things that we don't own into the objects of our future happiness instead of God. And for a believer, it's a step out of fellowship with God. That's because every potential target of lust—whether it's a young coworker, a film actress, a half-million-dollar house, or a sports car—can become an obsession; an idol in your heart.

Lust always restlessly wants more. "What is the source of the wars and the fights among you? Don't they come from the cravings that are at war within you?" (James 4:1 HCSB). Regardless of how amazing or appealing your spouse is, lust will make you dissatisfied with them. Lust fuels anger, numbs hearts, and destroys marriages. Rather than fullness, it leads to emptiness.

It's time to expose lust for what it really is—a misguided thirst for satisfaction that only God can fulfill. Lust is like a warning light on the dashboard of your heart, alerting you to the fact that you're not allowing God's love to fill you. When your eyes and heart are on Him, your actions will lead you to lasting joy, not to endless cycles of regret and condemnation.

"His divine power has granted to us everything pertaining to life and godliness, through the true knowledge of Him who called us by His own glory and excellence. For by these He has granted to us His precious and magnificent promises, so that by them you may become partakers of the divine nature, having escaped the corruption that is in the world by lust" (2 Peter 1:3–4). God isn't asking you to give up your lusts for nothing, leaving you with no comfort or adventure to take their place. He is not denying you pleasure; just redirecting you away from sinful and unsatisfying things to the pure and greater pleasures found in Him and in what He provides. He wants you to discover that nothing truly satisfies like Jesus.

What has been enticing and luring your eyes and heart away? What things in this world are you longing for as your next source of fulfillment? Can you admit you don't need them? Are you tired of being lied to by lust? Are you fed up with believing that forbidden pleasures are able to keep you happy and content—when you know they can't?

Then begin setting your heart back on God and partake of the feast of His Word. Let His promises of peace and freedom work their way into your heart. Confess any lust in your heart as sin, and allow the guilt and shame that weighs on you to be replaced by the joy of His forgiveness. Daily receive the unconditional love He has already proven to you through the cross. Focus on being grateful for everything God has already given you rather than choosing discontentment.

You'll find yourself so full on what He provides, you won't be hungry anymore for the junk food of lust.

And while you're at it, set your eyes and heart on your spouse again. "Rejoice in the wife of your youth. . . . Be exhilarated always with her love. For why should you, my son, be exhilarated with an adulteress and embrace the bosom of a foreigner? For the ways of a man are before the eyes of the Lord, and He watches all his paths" (Proverbs 5:18–21).

"Do not love the world nor the things in the world. If anyone loves the world, the love of the Father is not in him" (1 John 2:15). Lust is the best this world has to offer, but love offers you the best life in the world.

TODAY'S DARE

END IT NOW. IDENTIFY ANY OBSESSION
OR OBJECT OF LUST IN YOUR LIFE AND LET
GO OF IT. EXPOSE ANY LIE YOU'VE SWALLOWED
IN PURSUING FORBIDDEN PLEASURE AND
REJECT IT. LUST CANNOT BE ALLOWED TO
LIVE IN A BACK CLOSET. IT MUST BE KILLED
AND DESTROYED TODAY. FOCUS ON THANKING
GOD THAT HE AND WHAT HE PROVIDES CAN
SATISFY YOU AND MEET ALL YOUR NEEDS.

__ Check here when you've completed today's dare.

What did you identify as an area of lust? What has this
pursuit cost you over time? How has it led you away from the
person you want to be? Write about your new commitment
to seek Him—and to seek your spouse—rather than seeking
after foolish desires.

Act as free men, and do not use your freedom as a covering for evil. (1 Peter 2:16)

"I am so glad God put me through the Love Dare. It has made me a better man, a better father, a better husband."—Rich

DAY 25
Love forgives

What I have forgiven, if I have forgiven anything, I did it for your sakes in the presence of Christ. —*2 Corinthians 2:10*

This one is tough—perhaps the toughest dare in the book. But if there is to be any hope for your marriage, this is a challenge that must absolutely be taken seriously. Counselors and ministers who deal with broken couples will tell you that this is the most complex problem of all, a rupture that is often the last to be repaired. It cannot just be considered and contemplated but must be deliberately resolved. Forgiveness has to happen, or a successful marriage won't.

Jesus painted a vivid image of forgiveness in His parable of the ungrateful servant. He described a man who owed an overwhelming sum of money being surprised when his master totally canceled his debt. But upon release, the servant went out and found a poor man who owed him a small amount and mercilessly threw him in prison for not paying it. When the master heard of his lack of forgiveness, he confronted the servant and put the original debt back on him. "His lord, moved with anger, handed him over to the torturers until he should repay all that was owed him" (Matthew 18:34).

Torturers. Prison. When you think of unforgiveness, this is what should come to mind, for Jesus said, "My heavenly Father will also do the same to you, if each of you does not forgive his brother from your heart" (Matthew 18:35).

Imagine finding yourself in a prison-like setting. As you look around, you see a number of cells visible from where you're standing. You see people from your past incarcerated there—people who wounded you as a child. You see people you once called friends but who wronged you at some point in life. You might see one or both of your parents there, perhaps a sibling or some other family member. Even your spouse is locked in nearby, trapped with all the others in this jail of your own making.

This prison, you see, is a room in your own heart. This dark, drafty, depressing chamber exists inside you every day. But Jesus is standing nearby, extending to you a key that will release every inmate. He's telling you to forgive them all.

No. You don't want any part of it. These people have hurt you too badly. They knew what they were doing and yet they did it anyway—even your spouse, the one you should have been able to count on most of all. So you resist and turn away. You're unwilling to stay here any longer—seeing Jesus, seeing the key in His hand, knowing what He's asking you to do. It's just too much.

But in trying to escape, you make a startling discovery. There is no way out. You're trapped inside with all the other captives. Your unforgiveness, anger, and bitterness have made a prisoner of you as well. Like the servant in Jesus' story who was forgiven an impossible debt, you have chosen not to forgive and have been handed over to the jailers and torturers. Your own freedom is now dependent on your forgiveness.

Coming to this conclusion usually takes a while. You see all kinds of risks involved in forgiving others, since you feel what they did was wrong, whether they admit it or not. They may not even be sorry about it. They may feel perfectly justified in their actions, even going so far as to blame you for them.

But forgiveness doesn't absolve anyone of blame or clear their record with God. It just clears you of having to worry about how to punish them. When you forgive another person, you're not declaring them innocent. You're just turning them over to God, who can be counted on to deal with them His way. You're saving yourself the trouble of scripting any more arguments or trying to prevail in this situation. It's not about winning and losing anymore. It's about freedom. It's about letting go. Extending the mercy you have been given.

That's why you often hear people who have genuinely forgiven another person say, "It felt like a weight being lifted off my shoulders." Yes, that's exactly what it is. It's like a breath of fresh air rushing into your heart. The stale dankness of the prison house is flooded with light and coolness. For the first time in a long time, you feel at peace. You feel free.

But how do you do it? You release your anger and the responsibility for judging and punishing this person to the Lord. "Never take your own revenge, beloved, but leave room for the wrath of God, for it is written, 'Vengeance is Mine, I will repay,' says the Lord" (Romans 12:19). You might still feel the need to confront them about what they have done (Matthew 18:15), but regardless, forgiveness should go ahead and happen now.

How do you know you've done it? You know it when the thought of their name or the sight of their face, rather than causing your blood to boil, causes you to feel sorry for them instead, to genuinely hope they get this turned around.

Knowing that God is the Judge of all, Jesus said if we have anything against anyone, we should forgive (Mark 11:25)—and then *never stop* forgiving (Matthew 18:22). Bitterness will poison and drain the vitality out of any relationship.

So when it's all said and done, the romance, intimacy, and enjoyment of your marriage is greatly dependent upon your mutual commitment to allow *no* unforgiveness to exist between the two of you. Great marriages are not produced by people who never hurt each other, only by people who daily choose to keep "no record of wrongs" (1 Corinthians 13:5).

TODAY'S DARE

WHATEVER YOU HAVEN'T FORGIVEN IN YOUR
MATE, FORGIVE IT TODAY. LET IT GO. JUST AS
WE ASK JESUS TO "FORGIVE US OUR DEBTS"
EACH DAY, WE MUST ASK HIM TO HELP US
"FORGIVE OUR DEBTORS" EACH DAY AS WELL.
UNFORGIVENESS HAS BEEN KEEPING YOU AND
YOUR SPOUSE IN PRISON TOO LONG. SAY FROM
YOUR HEART, "I CHOOSE TO FORGIVE."

___ Check here when you've completed today's dare.

What did you forgive your spouse for today? How long
have you been carrying the weight of it? What are the possibili-
ties now that you've released this matter to God?

_____

_____

_____

_____

_____

_____

_____

Father, forgive them; for they do not know what they are doing. (Luke 23:34)

"We have forgiven each other and are starting over."—Andrea

DAY 26
Love is responsible

When you judge another, you condemn yourself, since you,
the judge, do the same things. —Romans 2:1 HCSB

God has designed His gift of marriage with many price-less benefits. Research shows that married people are happier, healthier, live longer, make more money, and have better sex lives. They also produce healthier, happier children than people who remain single. Do you realize how much value your spouse adds to your life? It's almost incomprehensible.

But as with anything in life, the benefits we enjoy in marriage depend on how responsible we are in taking good care of it. That's why taking personal responsibility is one of love's greatest requests. Unpopular, yes. But it is a key to whether marriage is a glorious union or a devastating failure.

Each marriage is a living garden placed under the care of husband and wife. Both of you. The more responsible you are to fulfill your vows, roles, and duties, the more you will enjoy the many delights and wonders of your oneness. But the less responsible you become, the more painful and divisive the consequences.

It is foolish, for example, for a man to desire healthy children and great intimacy in the bedroom, but not lift a finger to help his wife around the house or with training the kids. It is foolish for a woman to hope for financial stability and a happy marriage, but then spend without boundaries and refuse to meet her husband's sexual needs. Love and wisdom compel us not to neglect our responsibilities.

How about you? How are you doing with honoring what

you promised at the altar? Is your marriage blooming under your care, or wilting instead? Are you making your spouse carry all the weight, or are you looking for ways to lighten their load? Love calls us to take full responsibility for our partner in marriage. To love them. To cherish them. To help them.

But that's not all. Love also compels us to take responsibility for something else in our marriage: *our own mistakes.*

We are so quick to justify them. So quick to deflect criticism. To find fault with our spouse instead—who's always the closest target and easiest to blame. We tend to believe we are always more correct than they are. And we don't think anybody, given our same circumstances, would have acted much differently. But love doesn't pass the blame or justify wrongs. It doesn't make excuses. Instead, it faces reality about areas of personal weakness and failure that need to be willingly addressed.

So the next time you're in an argument with your spouse, stop and see if there's some truth to what he or she is saying. What might happen if instead of denying, blaming, and working up your comebacks, you humbly received their rebuke and took responsibility for your wrongs? The Scripture says, "Reprove a wise man and he will love you" (Proverbs 9:8). Love is wise and agreeable, willing to admit and correct its faults up front. To confess. To repent. To change. To hunger and thirst for a right relationship with each other again. This is love!

A real heart of repentance may take a while to grow in you. Pride is very resistant to responsibility. But humility and honesty before God and your spouse are crucial for a healthy relationship. This doesn't mean you're always in the wrong or that you should become a doormat. But if something is not right between you and your spouse or between you and God, making it right should be your first priority.

Are you taking responsibility for your own failures? Have you said or done things to your spouse that are wrong? What about to God? "If we say that we have no sin, we are deceiving ourselves and the truth is not in us," the Bible says (1 John 1:8). However, "if we confess our sins, He is faithful and righteous to forgive us our sins and to cleanse us from all unrighteousness" (1 John 1:9). Denial means living a lie, but we receive mercy from God at the point of our confession.

The same is true in marriage.

Apologies bring amazing breakthroughs. They can tear down walls of resistance, rebuild relational bridges, unclog pipelines of communication, and reignite feelings of affection. Even if your spouse is ninety percent wrong, the sooner you offer a genuine apology for your ten percent, the quicker the healing can begin and things can get back on track.

Can your spouse say that you have wronged or wounded them in any way and you've never made it right? If so, then it's time to humble yourself, be honest about your offenses, and repair the damage. *Think of it as an act of love.* God wants no unresolved issues left standing between the two of you. Ever. Ask Him to show you where you have fallen short in your responsibility, and get things right with Him first. Then once you've done that, get right with your spouse as well.

But to do this sincerely, you must swallow your pride and seek forgiveness, regardless of how your spouse responds. Your responsibility to courageously work through your own issues should not be affected by whether they choose to react kindly or coldly to you. This may be one of the most difficult things you've ever done, but it is crucial to taking the next step in your marriage and with God. If your heart is sincere, you may be surprised at the grace and strength He gives you when you take this step. Taking responsibility is always the loving thing to do.

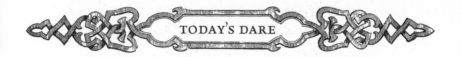

TODAY'S DARE

TAKE TIME TO PRAY THROUGH YOUR AREAS
OF RESPONSIBILITY AND YOUR AREAS OF
WRONGDOING. WHERE YOU HAVE FAILED,
ASK FOR GOD'S FORGIVENESS, THEN HUMBLE
YOURSELF ENOUGH TO ADMIT THEM TO YOUR
SPOUSE. DO IT SINCERELY AND TRUTHFULLY.
ASK YOUR SPOUSE FOR FORGIVENESS AS WELL.
NO MATTER HOW THEY RESPOND, MAKE SURE
YOU COVER YOUR RESPONSIBILITY IN LOVE.

___ Check here when you've completed today's dare.

How did your mate react to your apology? What does he
or she need to see in order to believe that your confession was
more than just words?

_____

_____

_____

_____

_____

_____

_____

Each one must examine his own work . . . in regard to himself alone. (Galatians 6:4)

"If you would've asked me a year ago if I wanted to be with her, I would've told you I'm leaving the past behind me. But God has showed me what pure love is."—Chris

DAY 27
Love encourages

Guard my soul and deliver me; do not let me be ashamed,
for I take refuge in You. —Psalm 25:20

Marriage has a way of altering our vision. We go in expecting our mate to fulfill our hopes and make us happy. But this is an impossible order to fill. So our unrealistic expectations breed disappointment. The higher your expectations, the more likely your spouse will fail you and cause you frustration.

If a wife always expects her husband to be on time, read her mind, and understand all her needs . . . if he always expects her to look radiant, blindly support his decisions, and stay emotionally ready for sex . . . both of them will set each other up for daily failure. They will likely live most of their married lives in constant disappointment. But if they are realistic enough to understand that their spouse is human, occasionally forgetful, and sometimes weak and thoughtless, they'll be more delighted when their mate *is* responsible, loving, and kind.

Divorce is nearly inevitable when people refuse to allow their spouses to be human. So make a transition in your thinking. Choose to live by *encouragement* rather than *expectations*.

The way your spouse has been for the last ten years is probably what he or she will be like in the future apart from your loving encouragement and an intervention from God. That's why love puts the focus on personal responsibility and improving ourselves rather than on demanding more from others.

Jesus painted a picture of this when He said, "How can you say to your brother, 'Let me take the speck out of your eye,' and behold, the log is in your own eye? You hypocrite, first take the log out of your own eye, and then you will see clearly to take the speck out of your brother's eye" (Matthew 7:4–5).

Does your spouse feel like they're living with a speck inspector? Are they routinely on edge, fearful of not living up to your expectations? Would they say they spend most days sensing more of your disapproval than your acceptance?

Perhaps you'd respond by saying that the problem is not with you but with them. If they really do come up short in a lot of areas, why is that your fault? As far as you're concerned, it takes both of you doing everything you can for your marriage to work. Your mate may think you're overly critical, but you feel the issues you bring up are legitimate. You're not saying you're perfect, but it seems like you should be able to point out genuine problem areas. Right?

The problem with this mentality is that few people are able to respond to criticism with joyful inspiration. When it seems clear to your spouse that you're unhappy with them—whether by direct confrontation or the silent treatment—it's hard for them not to feel deflated instead of motivated.

After all, unlike any other friendship, your relationship began with both of you willingly bending over backwards to please the other. You never expected to reach the point where you think nearly everything they do is wrong and you're struggling at times with even *liking* this person.

When hopes are daily doused with cold reality, your natural reaction is to communicate ongoing frustration with them. But sadly, rather than this making them want to correct things, your disapproval only makes them want to walk away or dig in deeper.

Love is too smart for that. Instead of putting your mate in a position to rebel, love says to give them the grace and room to be themselves. Even if you're the goal-oriented type who places high demands on yourself, love calls you to lead by example but not to force those same standards on your mate's performance. Marriage is a relationship to be enjoyed and savored along the way. It's a unique friendship designed by God Himself where two people live together in flawed imperfection, yet deal with it by encouraging and building, not by exhausting and belittling.

The Bible says, "Encourage the exhausted, and strengthen the feeble" (Isaiah 35:3). "Encourage one another and build up one another. . . . Encourage the fainthearted, help the weak, be patient with everyone" (1 Thessalonians 5:11, 14).

Don't you want married life to be a place where you can enjoy free expression of who you are, growing within a safe environment that encourages you even when you fail? Your spouse does too. And your *love* gives them that privilege.

If your wife or husband has told you on more than one occasion that you make them feel beaten down and defeated, then you need to take those words to heart. You can either be a critical anchor holding them back or a complementary wing helping them soar. Being with you should recharge them and lower their stress level, not drain them and wear them out. God is not done with your spouse yet. So let Him work.

Stop expecting your mate to understand all you're thinking, desire all you're wanting, and accomplish all you're hoping. As much as they may wish they could, they can't. Instead, let them be inspired by your appreciation. Let them be empowered by your sincere prayers and your strategic praise. Focus on their strengths and point out what they are getting right. Let your words lift them to a new height. Then the person they're created by God to be may emerge with a new confidence and with a love that inspires you for years to come.

TODAY'S DARE

ELIMINATE THE POISON OF UNREALISTIC
EXPECTATIONS IN YOUR HOME. THINK OF ONE
OR TWO AREAS WHERE YOUR SPOUSE HAS TOLD
YOU THAT YOU'RE EXPECTING TOO MUCH,
AND TELL THEM YOU'RE SORRY FOR BEING SO
HARD ON THEM ABOUT IT. PRAISE THEM FOR
SOMETHING POSITIVE AND ASSURE THEM
OF YOUR UNCONDITIONAL LOVE.

___ Check here when you've completed today's dare.

When you place high expectations on your spouse that
they don't feel internally motivated to attain, what does that
tell you about yourself? What are some better ways to deal with
these disconnects? What things has your spouse recently done
well that you can point out and thank them for?

Let us consider how to stimulate one another to love and good deeds. (Hebrews 10:24)

"Use this book. Read it and keep reading it. It feels so good to give love again."—Mike

DAY 28
Love makes sacrifices

He laid down His life for us. We should also lay down
our lives for our brothers. —1 John 3:16 HCSB

Life can be hard. But what we usually mean is that *our* life
can be hard. We're the first to feel it when *we're* the ones being
mistreated or inconvenienced. We're quick to sulk when *we're*
the ones who feel deprived or unappreciated. When life is difficult for us, we notice.

But too often the only way we notice that life is hard for
our mate is when they start complaining about it. Then instead
of genuinely caring or rushing in to help, we might think they
just have a bad attitude. The pain and pressure *they're* under
don't register with us nearly the same way as *our* pain and
pressure. When we want to complain, we expect everyone to
understand and feel sorry for us.

This doesn't happen when love is at work. Love doesn't
have to be jarred awake by your mate's obvious signs of distress.
Before worries and troubles have begun to bury them, love has
already gone into action mode. It sees the weight beginning to
pile up and it steps in to help. That's because love invites you to
be sensitive to your spouse.

Love makes sacrifices. It keeps you so tuned in to what
your spouse needs that you often respond without being asked.
And when you don't notice ahead of time and must be told
what's happening, love responds to the heart of the problem.
Quickly and directly.

Even when your mate's stress comes out in words of personal accusation, love shows compassion rather than becoming

defensive. Love can look beyond a complaint and see a hurting person with an unmet need crying out for help. Love will then give strategically to meet that need. Instead of sitting around upset that they're not treating you the way you think they should, let love pick you up out of your self-pity and turn your attention toward discovering and meeting their hidden needs.

That's what Jesus did. "He laid down His life for us" to show us that "we should also lay down our lives" for others (1 John 3:16 HCSB). He taught us that the evidence of love is found in seeing a need in others, then doing all we can to satisfy it. "For I was hungry, and you gave Me something to eat; I was thirsty, and you gave Me something to drink; I was a stranger, and you invited Me in; naked, and you clothed Me; I was sick, and you visited Me; I was in prison, and you came to Me" (Matthew 25:35–36).

These are the types of needs you should be looking for in your wife or husband:

- Is he *"hungry"*—needing you sexually, even when you don't feel like it?
- Is she *"thirsty"*—craving the time and attention you seem able to give to everyone else?
- Does he feel like a *"stranger"*—insecure in his work, needing home to be a refuge and sanctuary?
- Is she *"naked"*—frightened or ashamed, desperate for the warm covering of your loving affirmation?
- Is he feeling *"sick"*—physically tired and needing you to help guard him from interruptions?
- Does she feel in *"prison"*—fearful and depressed, needing some safety and intervention?

Love is willing to make sacrifices to see that the needs of your spouse are given your very best effort and focus. When your mate is overwhelmed and under the gun, love calls you to set aside what seems so essential in your own life to help rescue them, even if it's merely the gift of a listening ear.

Often all they really need is just to talk their situation out. They need to see in your two attentive eyes that you truly care about what this is costing them, and you're serious about helping them seek answers. They need you to pray with them about what to do, and then keep following up to see how it's going.

The words "How are you doing?" and "How can I help you?" need to stay fresh on your lips.

The solutions may be simple and easy for you to handle, or they may be complex and expensive, requiring time, energy, and great effort. Either way, God will give you unique insights into the pressure your mate is under and unique abilities to step in and greatly reduce their level of stress. "Bear one another's burdens, and thereby fulfill the law of Christ" (Galatians 6:2). Jesus willingly took our problems on Himself. And He extends us daily grace to empower us to do it for others.

When the New Testament believers began to walk in love, their lives together were marked by sharing and sacrifice. Their heartbeat was to worship the Lord and to serve His people. "All those who had believed were together and had all things in common; and they began selling their property and possessions and were sharing them with all, as anyone might have need" (Acts 2:44–45). As Paul said to one of these churches in a later decade, "I will most gladly spend and be expended for your souls" (2 Corinthians 12:15). Lives that have been raised from death by Jesus' great sacrifice should be ready and willing to make small, daily sacrifices for those within our reach and in need of our love.

TODAY'S DARE

WHAT IS ONE OF THE GREATEST NEEDS IN YOUR SPOUSE'S LIFE RIGHT NOW? IS THERE A NEED YOU COULD LIFT FROM THEIR SHOULDERS TODAY BY A DARING ACT OF SACRIFICE ON YOUR PART? WHETHER THE NEED IS BIG OR SMALL, PURPOSE TO DO WHAT YOU CAN TO MEET THE NEED.

___ Check here when you've completed today's dare.

How much of your mate's stress is caused by your lack of concern or initiative? When you expressed a desire to help, how did they receive it? Are there other needs you could meet?

Come to Me, all who are weary and heavy-laden, and I will give you rest. (Matthew 11:28)

"I will go through another forty days, and another and another,
until I have this ingrained in my heart."—Marty

DAY 29
Love's motivation

Render service with a good attitude, as to the Lord and not to men.
—Ephesians 6:7 HCSB

It doesn't take long to discover that your mate will not always motivate your love. Many times they will *de-motivate* it. More often than you'd like, it will seem difficult to find the inspiration to demonstrate your love. They may not even receive it when you try to express it. That's simply the nature of life, even in fairly healthy marriages.

But although moods and emotions can create all kinds of moving motivational targets, one motivation is certain to stay in the same place all the time. It's this: When God is your reason for loving, your ability to love is guaranteed . . . because love comes from Him.

Think of it like this. When you were a child, your parents most likely established rules for you to follow. Your bedtime was at a certain hour. Your room had to be kept mostly clean. Your schoolwork needed to be finished before you could play. If you were like most people, you bent these rules as often as you obeyed them. And if not for the incentive of force and consequences, you might not have obeyed them much at all.

But sometime in childhood you might have been taught an idea like this—"Children, be obedient to your parents in all things, for this is well-pleasing to the Lord" (Colossians 3:20). At some level you began to realize that you didn't merely have your parents to answer to anymore. This was no longer a battle of wills between you and your mom or dad. This was now between you and God.

As it turns out, however, the relationship between parents and children is not the only thing enhanced by letting God become your driving motivation. Consider the following areas where pleasing Him should become our goal:

Work. "Do your work heartily, as for the Lord rather than for men" (Colossians 3:23).

Service. "Obey those who are your masters on earth, not with external service, as those who merely please men, but with sincerity of heart, fearing the Lord" (Colossians 3:22).

Everything. Work hard at "whatever you do . . . knowing that from the Lord you will receive the reward of the inheritance. It is the Lord Christ whom you serve" (Colossians 3:23–24).

Even marriage. "Wives, be subject to your husbands, as is fitting in the Lord" (Colossians 3:18). "Husbands, love your wives, just as Christ also loved the church and gave Himself up for her" (Ephesians 5:25).

This means the love you demonstrate in marriage should actually have one chief objective: *loving and honoring the Lord with devotion and sincerity.* Your role as a husband or wife will take on new focus and drive when you see it as an instrument for living out your love for God, when pleasing Him becomes the *why* behind *what* you do.

God's Word says we can love Him through the ways we treat, serve, and love other people (1 John 3:17; 4:11–21). So every loving thought, attitude, or action in your marriage can become another way for you to say "I love you" to God. The fact that it blesses your spouse in the process is simply a wonderful, additional benefit.

You may think your marriage or love for your spouse will suffer from making God your primary focus and your greatest delight. But quite the contrary, all of it will flourish as you draw closer to the One who created marriage and who loves your wife or husband infinitely more than you do.

This change of focus and perspective is very strategic and crucial for a Christian. Being able to wake up knowing that God is your source and supply—not only of your own needs but also those of your spouse—changes your whole reason for interacting graciously toward your mate. No longer is it this imperfect person deciding how much love you'll show them, but rather your omni-perfect God is using even a flawed person like yourself to bestow loving favor on another.

Has your wife become fairly hard to live with lately? Is her slowness at getting over a disagreement wearing on your patience? Then don't withhold your love just because she thinks differently from you. Love her "as to the Lord."

Is your husband tuning you out, not saying much, brooding over something he's not interested in sharing? Are you tired of him being so inconsiderate of you, not even responding to the children the way he needs to? Then don't battle back with silence and inattention. Love him anyway. "As to the Lord."

Love motivated by raw duty cannot hold out for very long. And love only motivated by ideal conditions can never be assured of sufficient oxygen to keep it breathing. But love that is lifted up as an offering to God never loses its anchor and is able to sustain itself when all other weather conditions have lost their ability to energize us.

Those who are fine with mediocre marriages can leave their love to chance and hope for the best. But if you are committed to giving your spouse the best love you possibly can, then shoot for love's unchanging motivation. Love that keeps God as its primary focus is unlimited in the heights it can attain. When you're not motivated to do it for *them*, do it for *Him*.

TODAY'S DARE

BEFORE YOU SEE YOUR SPOUSE AGAIN
TODAY, PRAY FOR THEM BY NAME AND FOR
THEIR NEEDS. WHETHER IT COMES EASY FOR
YOU OR NOT, SAY "I LOVE YOU," THEN EXPRESS
LOVE TO THEM IN SOME TANGIBLE WAY.
GO TO GOD IN PRAYER AGAIN, THANKING
HIM FOR GIVING YOU THE PRIVILEGE
OF LOVING THIS ONE SPECIAL PERSON—
UNCONDITIONALLY, THE WAY
HE LOVES BOTH OF YOU.

___ Check here when you've completed today's dare.

How will this change of motivation affect your relationship and reactions? What does this inspire you to do? What
does it inspire you to stop doing?

_____

_____

_____

_____

_____

_____

As for me and my house, we will serve the Lord. (Joshua 24:15)

"My prayer is to make every day a 'dare day.'"—Jerry

DAY 30
Love brings unity

Father, keep them in Your name, the name which You have given Me, that they may be one even as We are. —John 17:11

One of the most impressive things about the Bible is the way it is beautifully linked together, with consistent themes running throughout its sixty-six books, working in harmony to share God's redemptive plan from beginning to end. Though it interweaves His revelations to forty different authors over a span of 1,600 years, each with various backgrounds and skill levels, God sovereignly inspired His Word with one united voice. And He continues to powerfully speak through it today with perfect relevance without ever changing His message.

Unity. Togetherness. Oneness. These are the unshakable hallmarks of our God.

From the very beginning of time, we see His unity at work through the Trinity—Father, Son, and Holy Spirit. God the Father is there, creating the heavens and the earth. The Spirit is there as well, "moving over the surface of the waters" (Genesis 1:2). And the Son, "the radiance of His glory and the exact representation of His nature" (Hebrews 1:3), joins in speaking the world into existence. "Let Us make man in Our image, according to Our likeness" (Genesis 1:26). Us. Our. All three, always in perfect oneness of mind and purpose.

Centuries later we see Jesus, having come to earth as a man, rising from the waters of baptism as the Spirit descends upon Him like a dove, and the Father announces over this majestic scene, "This is My beloved Son, in whom I am well-pleased" (Matthew 3:17).

Father, Son, and Spirit are in pristine unity. They serve each other, love each other, and honor each other. Though perfect and unsurpassed, they rejoice when the other is praised. Though distinct, they are one, indivisible.

And because this relationship is so special—so representative of the vastness and grandeur of God—He has chosen to let us experience one aspect of it very personally. In the unique relationship of husband and wife, two distinct individuals are spiritually united into "one flesh" (Genesis 2:24). And "what God has joined together, let man not separate" (Mark 10:9 NIV).

In fact, this mystery is so compelling—and the love between husband and wife so intertwined and complete—God designed the imagery of marriage to reflect and explain His love for the church. The church (the Bride) is most satisfied when its Savior is worshipped and celebrated. Christ (the Bridegroom), who has given Himself up for her, is pleased and honored when He sees her "as a radiant church, without stain or wrinkle or any other blemish, but holy and blameless" (Ephesians 5:27 NIV). Both Christ and the church love and honor the other.

That's the beauty of *unity*. It always strengthens relationships and homes, while division always destroys them.

What would happen in your marriage, husband, if you devoted yourself to loving, honoring, and serving your wife in all things? What if you determined that the preservation of your oneness with this woman was worth every sacrifice and expression of love you could make? What if you wisely navigated through conversations and misunderstandings in such a way to guard the unity between you?

What would happen, wife, if you made it your mission to do everything possible to promote togetherness of heart with your husband? What if every threat to your unity was treated as a poison, a cancer, an enemy to be eliminated by the medicines of love, humility, respect, and selflessness? What would your marriage become if you were never again willing to see your oneness torn apart?

What if we took these words of the apostle Paul to heart? "Now I exhort you, brethren, by the name of our Lord Jesus Christ, that you all agree and that there be no divisions among you, but that you be made complete in the same mind and in the same judgment" (1 Corinthians 1:10).

Oneness in marriage requires keeping each other on the same page. It means communication must become constant so that union can be constantly enjoyed. It means sharing your thoughts, values, decisions, and upcoming plans, interweaving your lives together so that you maintain one heart, decide in one accord, and speak with one voice. And whenever anything or anyone disrupts your unity, you both quickly do whatever it takes to resolve it and restore it. To agree again.

The unity of the Trinity, as seen from beyond the reaches of history past and continuing on into the future, gives evidence to the power of oneness. It is unbreakable. It is unending. It is wonderful. And it is this same spiritual reality that disguises itself each day at your home and mailing address. Though painted in the colors of work schedules and doctor visits and trips to the grocery store, oneness is the eternal thread that runs through the daily experience of what we call "our marriage" and gives it a purpose to be defended for life.

Therefore, love this one who is as much a part of your body as you are. Serve this one whose needs cannot be separated from your own. Honor this one who, when raised upon the pedestal of your love, raises you both up as a clearer reflection of God, all at the same time.

TODAY'S DARE

ISOLATE ONE AREA OF DIVISION IN YOUR
MARRIAGE AND PRAY ABOUT IT. ASK THE LORD
TO REVEAL ANYTHING IN YOUR OWN HEART
THAT IS THREATENING ONENESS IN YOUR
MARRIAGE. PRAY THAT HE WOULD OPEN UP
THE COMMUNICATION LINES SO THAT YOU
CAN FIND MORE AGREEMENT AND STAY ON
THE SAME PAGE. AND IF APPROPRIATE,
DISCUSS THIS MATTER OPENLY,
SEEKING GOD FOR UNITY.

___ Check here when you've completed today's dare.

Did the Lord open your eyes to anything new that might
be giving fuel to this point of disagreement? How do you
intend to respond? What do you hope to see God do in your
spouse as well?

_____

_____

_____

_____

_____

_____

The Lord is our God, the Lord is one! (Deuteronomy 6:4)

"I want my children to know how great marriage can be
when God is in the center of it."—Lisa

DAY 31
Love and marriage

A man shall leave his father and his mother, and be joined to his wife;
and they shall become one flesh. —Genesis 2:24

This verse is God's original blueprint for marriage. His
specific "one man + one woman = one" design was established
at creation (Genesis 2:24), verified by Jesus (Mark 10:6–9), and
clarified by the apostle Paul (Ephesians 5:31). But for it to work
as designed, it requires a tearing away and a knitting together.
It reconfigures existing relationships while establishing a
brand new one. *Marriage changes everything.* And couples who
don't take this "leaving" and "cleaving" message to heart will
reap the consequences down the line, when the problems are
much harder to repair without hurting someone.

"Leaving" means that you are breaking a natural tie. Your
parents now step into the role of counselors to be respected,
but are no longer authorities who tell you what to do.

Many newlyweds, however, have a hard time leaving their
parents behind. Or parents may not feel ready to release a child
from their control and expectations, and fail to do their part in
this necessary transaction. In such cases, the grown child must
make "leaving" a courageous choice of his own. And far too
often, this break is not made in the right way.

The purpose of "leaving," of course, is not to abandon all
contact with the past but rather to establish and preserve the
unique oneness that marriage is designed to capture. Only
in oneness can you become all God means for you to be. If
you're too tightly bound to your parents, if they or your in-laws
are allowed to dictate and make demands, the independent

identity of your marriage that God desires will not be able to come to flower. You will always be held back, and a root of division will continue to send up weeds into your relationship.

You need to lovingly tell them that while you are grateful for their counsel and prayers, they must give you and your spouse the space to freely make your own decisions. Even if they react with surprise or a sense of hurt, this is a necessary step to help you move forward together. Courage and clarity must be gently employed to break your marriage free from any unhealthy attachment.

Sometimes, the unhealthy ties that parents keep with their children are related to unfinished business. Dad may feel that an apology is still in order or a wrong hasn't been forgiven. Mom may fear that her grown child won't survive without her. They may both be feeling insecurity in adjusting to the empty nest. They may simply long to be thanked for all they've done or need assurance of your continued love. Regardless, the married son or daughter is wise to take his or her parents out for a meal or write them a well-thought-out letter to express genuine love and grateful appreciation along with any needed words of apology or encouragement.

Just know that issues likely won't go away unless you do something. Your greater loyalty must shift from your parents to your spouse. It must also shift away from old flames and old friends to your mate. Everyone else must take a back seat and become properly emotionally distanced enough to give your union room to bloom. For without "leaving," you cannot do the "cleaving" you need, the joining of your hearts that's required to experience oneness.

"Cleaving" carries the idea of catching someone by pursuit, clinging to them as your new help and support. This union should form a oneness that can benefit everything else you do.

This man is now the spiritual leader of your new home, tasked with the responsibility of providing for you, protecting you, and loving you "just as Christ also loved the church and gave Himself up for her" (Ephesians 5:25). This woman is now one in union with you, called to help, beautifully complete, and uniquely support you as one who chooses to respect her husband the way the church respects Christ (Ephesians 5:22–33). Both of you raise your marriage exponentially in value the more you realize whom you are called to daily represent.

However, it's not unusual for couples—even Christian couples—to think they know better than God does and ignore His purpose for their union or their roles as He designed. Applying Genesis 2:24 seems too foreign or difficult for them. So they settle for worldly thinking and neglect the "leaving and cleaving" God intended. They may sacrifice the oneness and strength of the most ultimate relationship of their lives to please others who are not a part of them. They don't realize that the more unified their marriage, the more fulfilled and stronger they will be to handle every other role and responsibility in their lives.

It's extremely hard, of course, when your pursuit of oneness is basically one-sided. Your spouse may not currently be interested in recapturing the unity and purpose in your marriage that God has printed on its DNA. Even if there is a measure of desire on their part, the divisive issues between the two of you may be nowhere close to being resolved.

But by praying for and prioritizing your mate above your other loyalties, by protecting your oneness as a guarded treasure, your marriage over time can begin to enjoy the majesty of unity that God intended. His decision to make you "one" in marriage was intentional, beautiful, eternal, and can make anything possible.

So leave. And cleave. And dare to walk as one.

IS THERE A "LEAVING" ISSUE WITH YOUR PARENTS OR SOMEONE ELSE YOU HAVEN'T BEEN BRAVE ENOUGH TO CONQUER YET? CONFESS IT TO YOUR SPOUSE TODAY, AND RESOLVE TO MAKE IT RIGHT. THE ONENESS OF YOUR MARRIAGE IS DEPENDENT UPON IT. FOLLOW THIS WITH A COMMITMENT TO YOUR SPOUSE AND TO GOD TO MAKE YOUR MARRIAGE THE TOP PRIORITY OVER EVERY OTHER HUMAN RELATIONSHIP.

__ Check here when you've completed today's dare.

Has this been a hard thing for you to deal with? How has it affected your relationship? If the worse offender in this area is your spouse (with your in-laws), how can you lovingly move this toward a better situation?

May they all be one, as You, Father, are in Me and I am in You. (John 17:21 HCSB)

"We have learned so much about each other in these forty days. We have learned to love unconditionally, take time for each other, and grow spiritually together."—Paula

DAY 32
Love meets sexual needs

The husband must fulfill his duty to his wife, and likewise
also the wife to her husband. —1 Corinthians 7:3

In marriage, romance is meant to thrive and vibrantly flourish. Both the Old and New Testaments commend the beauty of sexual love within the context of matrimony.

The Song of Solomon, for example, though frequently misunderstood as nothing more than an allegory about God's passion for His people, is also a beautiful love story. It describes sexual acts between a husband and wife in beautiful, poetic detail, showing us how each spouse can passionately love and cherish the other in their romantic relationship.

In some of his other writings, Solomon said, "Let your fountain be blessed, and rejoice with the wife of your youth. As a loving deer and a graceful doe, let her breasts satisfy you at all times; and always be enraptured with her love" (Proverbs 5:18–19 NKJV). Words like these—"blessed," "rejoice," "satisfy," "enraptured"—vividly remind us that sexual intimacy is one of God's greatest wedding gifts, to be fully enjoyed on a consistent basis as husband and wife.

It is all part of celebrating what God has so graciously given to us in each other—the purity of being "naked and unashamed" (Genesis 2:25) within the covenant of our lifelong commitment. Through the pleasure of physical intimacy, we experience a strengthening of our relational, emotional, and spiritual intimacy as well. Faithful love transitions into overwhelming joy, resulting in a deep, abiding peace that no other sexual relationship outside of marriage can ever produce. As part of our married union, sex has no cost, no guilt, and no regrets.

This is why God approves of only *one* sexual relationship—one man and one woman who are married to one another—and why He has placed around it such loving, protective boundaries. By proclaiming that "marriage is to be held in honor among all, and the marriage bed is to be undefiled" (Hebrews 13:4), God provides us with the only way to protect our moral purity (1 Corinthians 7:1–2), protect our bodies physically (1 Corinthians 6:18), honor our spouse faithfully (Exodus 20:14), and keep our sexual experiences glorifying to Him (1 Corinthians 6:19). He is not limiting our enjoyment but protecting it . . . and us.

But we are weak. Affected by our past. Deceived by our culture. Tempted by unholy desires. Some Christians secretly view sex in their marriages as dirty or shameful. Some are haunted and weighed down by memories of immorality and adultery in their past. Some have given in to the destructive undertow of pornography, fueling their lusts with man-made, sinful alternatives to the pure, unpolluted, replenishing experience God designed our sexual oneness to be. As a result, many husbands and wives have grown distant from each other, allowing staleness to set in, pushing each other away, withholding something precious that rightly and exclusively belongs to their spouse.

God established marriage with a "one flesh" mentality (Genesis 2:24). "The wife does not have authority over her own body, but the husband does; and likewise also the husband does not have authority over his own body, but the wife does" (1 Corinthians 7:4). You are "one" and belong to each other. You are the sole person on the face of the earth called and designated by God to meet your spouse's sexual needs.

So "stop depriving one another," the Bible warns, "except by agreement for a time, so that you may devote yourselves to prayer, and come together again so that Satan will not tempt you because of your lack of self-control" (1 Corinthians 7:5). If your spouse comes knocking and requesting physical intimacy, your love should open the door and welcome them in. Sex (or the withholding of it) is not to be used as a weapon or bargaining chip. The heart of marriage is one of giving ourselves to each other to meet the other's needs.

"You have been bought with a price" (1 Corinthians 6:20). God set His affections on you and has gone to every length to draw you into desiring Him. Now it's your turn to pay the loving price to win the heart of your mate. Sex is one God-given opportunity to practice what the Love Dare entails.

But in reality, it is even more than that.

The greatest celebration of all time will occur when those who know and love Jesus Christ enter heaven to be with Him forever. It will be the consummation of our covenant of salvation, when the Bride of Christ, the Church, will finally be with her beloved Bridegroom (Ephesians 5:21–32). Though heaven is not described as being sexual, God gives us a small taste of heavenly joy through the regular physical consummation of the covenant between a husband and wife. The temporary joy we feel during sexual climax should cause us to worship God with hope and anticipation of the greater and purer joys that will forever be ours in heaven.

So each time you consummate your sacred relationship as husband and wife, remember that your union is a celebration of your marital intimacy, the grand finale of your mutual love. Even more importantly, it is for the beautiful glory of your holy God. Worship Him with your oneness for what He's done and for the eternal joy that's soon to come!

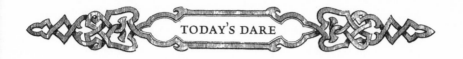

TODAY'S DARE

IF AT ALL POSSIBLE, TRY TO INITIATE SEX WITH
YOUR HUSBAND OR WIFE TODAY. DO THIS IN
A WAY THAT HONORS WHAT YOUR SPOUSE HAS
TOLD YOU (OR IMPLIED TO YOU) ABOUT WHAT
THEY NEED FROM YOU SEXUALLY. ASK GOD
TO MAKE THIS ENJOYABLE FOR BOTH OF YOU
AS WELL AS A PATH TO GREATER INTIMACY.

___ Check here when you've completed today's dare.

Was this a satisfying experience for you? If it didn't turn
out the way you'd hoped, what do you think is complicating
matters? Have you committed this to prayer? If it was a true
blessing for both of you, what can you learn from this for the
future?

_____

_____

_____

_____

_____

_____

For "Seven Steps to Better Sex," see the Appendix, page 224.

How beautiful and how delightful you are, my love. (Song of Solomon 7:6)

DAY 33
Love completes each other

If two lie down together they keep warm,
but how can one be warm alone? —Ecclesiastes 4:11

In the finale of God's creation, He made the first marriage
by taking one man, removing part of him, and fashioning a
woman. In this mystery of matrimony, two could then come
together and become one. Adam, though complete with God
alone, found his God-given needs met even more fully with
Eve, his complement in life. This is true in your marriage also.
Although love must be willing to act alone if necessary, it is
always better when it is not just a solo performance.

Our bodies, for example, are made for each other. Our
natures and temperaments provide balance, enabling us to
more effectively complete the tasks before us. Our oneness can
produce children, and our teamwork as a mom and dad can
best raise them to health and maturity.

Where one is weak, the other is strong. When one needs
building up, the other is equipped to enhance him, to encourage her. We can multiply one another's joys and divide one
another's sorrows.

"Two are better than one," the Scriptures wisely say,
"because they have a good return for their labor. For if either
of them falls, the one will lift up his companion. But woe
to the one who falls when there is not another to lift him
up" (Ecclesiastes 4:9–10). Your two hands don't just coexist
together; they multiply the effectiveness of the other. And to
continue succeeding at this level, each is not complete without
the other.

The Lord knew before you were born that you would one day marry your mate. And in His design of your gender differences, personalities, birth order, family origin, and uniqueness, He intentionally created needs in both of you that the other would be exclusively designed to meet. Although these differences can frequently be the source of misunderstanding and conflict, they have been created by God to be ongoing blessings if we respect them.

One of you may be better at cooking, while the other is better at cleaning the dishes. She may be more gentle and able to keep peace among family members, while he might handle confrontation and discipline more effectively. He may have a good business head but needs his wife to help him remember to be generous. When we learn to accept these distinctions in our mate, we can bypass criticism and go straight to helping and appreciating one another.

But some can't seem to get past them. They can't tolerate their mate's differences. And they suffer many wasted opportunities as a result. They don't take advantage of the uniqueness that makes each of them more effective when including the other.

One such example from the Bible is Pontius Pilate, the Roman governor who presided over the trial of Jesus. Unaware of who Christ was, he allowed the crowd to influence him into crucifying Jesus. But the one person who was more sensitive to what was happening was Pilate's own wife, who came to him and warned him. "While he was sitting on the judgment seat, his wife sent him a message, saying, 'Have nothing to do with that righteous Man; for last night I suffered greatly in a dream because of Him'" (Matthew 27:19).

She was apparently a woman of keen discernment who grasped the magnitude of these events before her husband did. Granted, God's sovereignty was at work, and nothing would have kept His Son from going to the cross for us. But Pilate's dismissal of his wife's intuition reveals an unfortunate side of man's nature that is often downplayed. God made wives to complete their husbands. He gives them insight that in many cases is kept from their men. If this discernment is ignored, it is usually to the detriment of the man making the decision.

When God looked at Adam and said, "I will make a helper suitable for him" (Genesis 2:18), the Creator knew what He was doing. He knew that men need help. They try to function alone but consistently fall short. So a wife's title as "helper" to her husband is a high compliment, not a second-class label or in any way a criticism. In fact, God Himself is referred to as our Helper (Psalm 124:8). Jesus called the Holy Spirit a Helper (John 14:26). A husband who has a wife willing to help him fulfill God's assignments for his life has a priceless treasure.

Marriage is one of God's unique ways of showing both men and women that we're not all-sufficient in ourselves, that the effectiveness of our marriage is dependent upon both of us working together. Do you have big decisions to make about your finances or retirement planning? Are you grappling with the appropriate action to take about a work situation? Are you absolutely convinced that your educational choices for the children are right, no matter what your spouse thinks?

Don't try doing all the analysis yourself. Don't disqualify your spouse's importance in voicing an opinion on matters that affect both of you. Love realizes that God has put you together on purpose. And though you may wind up disagreeing with your spouse's perspectives, you should still give their views respect and strong consideration. This honors God's design for your relationship and guards the oneness He intends. Joined together, you are greater than your independent parts. You need each other. You complete each other.

TODAY'S DARE

RECOGNIZE THAT YOUR SPOUSE IS
INTEGRAL TO YOUR FUTURE SUCCESS.
LET THEM KNOW TODAY THAT YOU DESIRE
TO INCLUDE THEM IN YOUR UPCOMING
DECISIONS, AND THAT YOU NEED THEIR
PERSPECTIVE AND COUNSEL. IF YOU
HAVE IGNORED THEIR INPUT IN THE
PAST, ADMIT YOUR OVERSIGHT AND
ASK THEM TO FORGIVE YOU.

___ Check here when you've completed today's dare.

How did your spouse respond? What are some upcoming
decisions you can make together? What did you learn today
about the role of your mate?

_____

_____

_____

_____

_____

_____

_____

Put on love, which is the perfect bond of unity. (Colossians 3:14)

"I feel like we are more 'in love' now, more than just 'committed.'"—Alice

DAY 34
Love celebrates godliness

[Love] does not rejoice in unrighteousness,
but rejoices with the truth. —1 Corinthians 13:6

The closer you and your spouse are to God, the more loving you will be in marriage (John 13:34–35). Our roles as husband or wife are greatly enhanced by becoming growing Christians. People who don't rely on God are significantly limited, left to depend on their own changing feelings, selfish thinking, and human efforts. But *with* Him, we have daily access to His toolbox for marriage. His Word nourishes us spiritually and equips us (2 Timothy 3:16–17). His counsel guides our thoughts and decisions with wisdom (James 1:5). His Holy Spirit works to improve our attitudes and mature us from the inside out (Galatians 5:22–25). Every act of hatred, every subtle deception, and every plot of unfaithfulness is vetoed by His love.

But on those days when we—even as believers—refuse to prayerfully depend upon Him, walk in His love, or obey His commands, we can become spiritually dry. Pride and selfishness can begin to take over. Anger, impatience, and thoughtlessness can become our default. Then our spouses and families are left to deal with the fallout.

Walking in fellowship with God is better than a thousand marriage books or counseling sessions, as helpful as these resources can be. Men who are walking closely with God each day won't deceive or degrade their wives. When God is guiding a woman's mouth, she will encourage her family instead of complaining or tearing them down. Simply put, one of the greatest priorities for your marriage should be daily cultivating your relationship with God while celebrating any spiritual growth in your spouse.

What makes you the proudest of your husband? What overjoys you the most in your wife? Is it when he wins at golf or she finds a great deal at the mall? Or are you most impressed when he gathers the family to pray and read the Word before bed, or when she forgives the neighbor whose dog dug up some of your plants? You are one of the most influential people in your spouse's life. They will want to please whoever praises them the most. Have you been using your influence to lead them to honor God?

Love rejoices most in the things that please God. When your mate is growing in Christian character, persevering in faith, seeking purity, and embracing roles of giving and service—becoming spiritually active in your home—the Bible says you should be celebrating it. More than when they save money on the grocery bill. More than when they achieve success at work.

It should be romantic for a woman to see her strong husband humbling himself before God. It should be inspiring for a man to see his wife living with deep spiritual conviction and passion. You should rejoice and be absolutely thrilled, excitedly cheering them on for what they're allowing God to accomplish in their lives.

The apostle Paul often wrote in his letters how delighted he was to hear reports of people's faithfulness and growth in Jesus. "We ought always to give thanks to God for you, brethren, as is only fitting, because your faith is greatly enlarged, and the love of each one of you toward one another grows ever greater; therefore, we ourselves speak proudly of you among the churches of God" (2 Thessalonians 1:3–4).

Sometimes, by accepting modern culture's take on what to applaud in our spouse, we can actually be guilty of encouraging them to sin, perhaps by feeding their vanity or by letting boys be boys. But "love does not rejoice in unrighteousness"—not in ourselves, and not in our mate. Rather, love "rejoices with the truth," the way the apostle John did when he said, "I have no greater joy than this, to hear of my children walking in the truth" (3 John 4). He knew that the pursuit of godliness, purity, and faithfulness—remaining unjaded and uncompromising in life—was the only way for them to please God, complete their purpose, and find joy and fulfillment in life.

But what if your spouse is not a believer? How can you champion godly behavior in them if they don't believe in God and refuse to submit to Him? Paul told believing spouses to stay true to their unbelieving mates, pray for them, and live an exemplary life before them in reverence to God (1 Corinthians 7:10–16). Yes, this may invite ridicule in some marriages. But when Christ takes over a man's heart, the long-term life change and spiritual transformation God develops in him is a powerful testimony that is hard for his wife to deny. Scripture exhorts wives to quietly use their submission, purity, and respectful behavior to win over their husbands (1 Peter 3:1–2). Sometimes you may feel as if you are only making it more difficult for your spouse to see Jesus in you. But stay prayerful, respectful, and loving. God is not finished with them yet. He has placed a witness to Himself right in their bed next to them.

What more could you want for your wife or husband than for them to experience the best that life has to offer—the best that God has to offer! So, yes, be encouraged and happy for any success your spouse enjoys. But save your heartiest congratulations for those times when they are taking closer steps to God and honoring Him as their First Love.

TODAY'S DARE

FIND A SPECIFIC, RECENT EXAMPLE WHEN YOUR SPOUSE DEMONSTRATED CHRISTIAN CHARACTER IN A NOTICEABLE WAY (FAITH, LOVE, HONESTY, PATIENCE, KINDNESS, SERVICE, COMPASSION, HUMILITY, ETC.). VERBALLY COMMEND THEM FOR THIS AT SOME POINT TODAY.

___ Check here when you've completed today's dare.

What example did you choose to recognize? How many other ways could you celebrate their growth in godliness? How could you encourage them to persevere in it?

I will walk within my house in the integrity of my heart. (Psalm 101:2)

"*Where would I be without this book and the way
God has moved through these dares each day?*"—Linda

DAY 35
Love is accountable

Plans fail for lack of counsel, but with many advisers they succeed.
—*Proverbs 15:22* NIV

Mighty sequoia trees tower hundreds of feet in the air and can withstand intense environmental pressures. Lightning can strike them, fierce winds can blow, and forest fires can rage around them. But the sequoia endures, standing firm, only growing stronger through the trials.

One of the secrets to the strength of this giant tree is what goes on below the surface. Unlike many trees, they reach out and interlock their roots with the sequoias around them. Each becomes empowered and reinforced by the strength of the others.

The secret to the sequoia is also a key to maintaining a strong, healthy marriage. A couple that faces problems alone is more likely to fall apart during tough times. However, the ones who interlock their lives in a network of other strong marriages radically increase their chances of surviving the fiercest of storms. It is crucial that a husband and wife pursue godly advice, healthy friendships, and experienced mentors.

Everyone needs wise counsel throughout life. Wise people constantly seek it and gladly receive it. Fools never ask for it and then ignore it when it's given to them.

As the Bible so clearly explains, "The way of a fool is right in his own eyes, but a wise man is he who listens to counsel" (Proverbs 12:15).

Gaining wise counsel is like having a detailed road map and a personal guide while traveling on a long, challenging journey. It can be the difference between continual success or the destruction of another marriage. It is vital that you invite strong couples to share the wisdom they have gained through their own successes and failures.

Why waste years of your life learning painful lessons when you could discover those same truths during a few hours of wise counsel? Why not cross the bridges others have built? Wisdom is more valuable than gold. Not receiving it is like letting priceless coins pass through your fingers.

Good marriage mentors warn you before you make a bad decision. They encourage you when you are ready to give up. And they cheer you on as you reach new levels of intimacy in your marriage.

Do you have an older couple or a friend of the same gender you can turn to for good advice, for prayer support, and for regular accountability check-ups? Do you have someone in your life who shoots straight with you?

You and your spouse need these types of friends and mentors on a consistent basis. The Bible says, "Encourage one another day after day . . . so that none of you will be hardened by the deceitfulness of sin" (Hebrews 3:13). Too often we can isolate ourselves from others. If we are not careful, we could push away the people who love us the most.

You must guard yourself against the wrong influencers. Everyone has an opinion and some people will encourage you to act selfishly and leave your mate in order to pursue your own happiness. Be careful about listening to advice from people who don't have a good marriage themselves.

If your marriage is hanging by a thread or already heading for a divorce, then you need to stop everything and pursue solid counseling as quickly as possible. Call a pastor, a Bible-believing counselor, or a marriage ministry today. As awkward as it may initially be to open up your life to a stranger, your marriage is worth every second spent and every sacrifice you will make for it. Even if your marriage is fairly stable, you're in no less need of honest, open mentors—people who can put wind in your sails and make your marriage even better.

How do you pick a good mentor? You look for a person who has the kind of marriage you want. You look for a person whose heart for Christ comes first before everything else. You look for someone who doesn't live by his or her opinions but by the unchanging Word of God. And more times than not, this person will likely be delighted you asked for help. Start praying for God to send this person into your life. Then pick a time to meet and talk.

If this doesn't sound too important to you, it would be a good idea to ask yourself why. Do you have something to hide? Are you afraid you will be embarrassed? Do you think your marriage is exempt from needing outside help? Does diving into a river of positive influence not appeal to you? Don't be the captain of another Titanic divorce by ignoring the warning signs around you when you could have been helped.

Here's an important reminder from Scripture: "Each one of us will give an account of himself to God" (Romans 14:12). This appointment is unbreakable. And though we're all ultimately responsible for the way we approach it, we can surely stand as much help as others can give. It might just be the relational influence that takes your marriage from mediocre to amazing.

FIND A MARRIAGE MENTOR—SOMEONE WHO
IS A STRONG CHRISTIAN AND WHO WILL BE
HONEST AND LOVING WITH YOU. IF YOU FEEL
THAT COUNSELING IS NEEDED, THEN TAKE
THE FIRST STEP TO SET UP AN APPOINTMENT.
DURING THIS PROCESS, ASK GOD TO DIRECT
YOUR DECISIONS AND DISCERNMENT.

___ Check here when you've completed today's dare.

Who did you choose? Why did you select this person?
What do you hope to learn from them?

In abundance of counselors there is victory. (Proverbs 11:14)

"I said, 'Nothing can fix what's already this broken.' But God has removed everything that was contaminating our marriage."—Shannon

DAY 36
Love is God's Word

Your word is a lamp to my feet and a light to my path.
—Psalm 119:105

The Bible is the most beloved and powerful book of all time. It was the first book ever published, is translated into more languages than any other in history, and remains the best seller of all best sellers. No book has enlightened so much darkness, educated so much ignorance, propagated so much love, reprimanded so much evil, or predicted the future so accurately as the Bible. It not only explains our origins and purpose for life, but how we can know God here and in eternity beyond the grave.

For some people, the Bible seems just too big to understand. They don't know where or how to begin. But as a Christian, you're not left alone to try grasping the major themes and deep meanings of the Bible. The Holy Spirit, who now lives in your heart by way of salvation, is an illuminator of truth. "For the Spirit searches all things, even the depths of God" (1 Corinthians 2:10). And because of His internal lamp, the Scriptures are now yours to read, absorb, comprehend, and live by.

But first, you've got to commit to do it.

Be in it. If this is not already a habit of yours, now is the time to begin reading a portion of the Bible every day. Ideally, read it together as husband and wife—in the morning, perhaps, or before bed. Be like the writer of Psalm 119, who could say, "With all my heart I have sought You. . . . Your word I have treasured in my heart, that I may not sin against You" (Psalm 119:10–11). Those who practice a consistent pattern of reading the Bible soon discover it to be "more desirable than gold, yes, than much fine gold; sweeter also than honey and the drippings of the honeycomb" (Psalm 19:10).

Stay under it. Yes, the Bible can be deep and challenging. That's why it's so important to be part of a church where the Word is faithfully taught and preached. By hearing it explained in sermons and Bible study groups, you'll get a broader, more balanced view of what God is saying through His Word. You'll also get to join with others who are on the same journey you are, wanting to be fed by the truths of Scripture. "Continue in the things you have learned and become convinced of, knowing from whom you have learned them" (2 Timothy 3:14).

Live it. Unlike most other books, which are only designed to be read and digested, the Bible is a living book. It lives because the Holy Spirit still resonates within its words. It lives because, unlike the ancient writings of other religions, its Author is still alive. And it lives because it becomes a part of who you are, how you think, and what you do. "Prove yourselves doers of the word, and not merely hearers" (James 1:22).

Jesus talked about people who build their lives on sand. They hear the truth of God's Word, but they ignore it and go their own way instead. When the storms of life begin to blow, foundations of sand will only result in total disaster. Their houses may light up and look nice for a while, but they are tragedies waiting to happen. Ultimately they collapse.

But Jesus said, "Everyone who hears these words of Mine and acts on them, may be compared to a wise man who built his house on the rock. The rain fell, and the floods came, and the winds blew and slammed against that house; and yet it did not fall, for it had been founded on the rock" (Matthew 7:24–25). When your home is founded on the rock of God's unchanging Word, it is insured against destruction. That's because God has exactly the right plan for everything, and

He's revealed these plans in His Word. They're right there for anyone who will simply read and apply them.

God has a better plan for the way you handle your money, for example. A wiser plan for the way you raise your children. A healthier plan for the way you treat your body. A more productive plan for the way you spend your time. A more loving, peaceful plan for the way you handle conflict. Isn't it just like your Maker to know exactly what you need?

If being a regular Bible reader is new for you, you'll be surprised how quickly you'll begin thinking differently and more eternally once you start. And if you're serious about establishing strategies for life based on God's way of doing things, He will guide you to make connections between what you're reading and how it applies. It's an enlightening journey with discoveries to be made all the time. In it, you will discover the secrets to handling wisely the issues of life. The most important truths of the Love Dare were discovered while reading God's Word.

Every area of life that you submit to His guidance and wisdom will grow stronger and more long-lasting over time. But any facet you withhold from Him, choosing instead to go your own way, will weaken and eventually fail when the storms of life hit you. That one part may, in fact, be the one area that could hasten the downfall of your home and marriage. May God help you to trust His Word completely even when you don't fully understand it. It will not fail you.

Wise couples build their houses on the rock of God's Word. They've seen what sand can do. They know how it feels when their footing gets soft and the foundation gives way. That's why you must determine to build your life and marriage on the solid rock of the Bible, and then you can plan on a stronger future—no matter how bad the storms get.

TODAY'S DARE

COMMIT TO READING THE BIBLE
EVERY DAY. FIND A DEVOTIONAL BOOK
OR OTHER RESOURCE THAT WILL GIVE YOU
SOME GUIDANCE. IF YOUR SPOUSE IS OPEN TO
IT, SEE IF THEY WILL COMMIT TO DAILY BIBLE
READING WITH YOU. BEGIN SUBMITTING
EACH AREA OF YOUR LIFE TO ITS GUIDANCE,
AND START BUILDING ON THE ROCK.

___ Check here when you've completed today's dare.

What parts of your life are in the greatest need of God's
counsel? Where do you feel the most susceptible to failure?
What are you asking God to show you through His Word?

For a way to familiarize yourself with the Bible, see the Appendix, page 227.

Whatever was written in earlier times was written for our instruction. (Romans 15:4)

Day 37
Love agrees in prayer

If two of you agree on earth about anything that they may ask,
it shall be done for them by My Father. —Matthew 18:19

If someone told you that by changing one specific thing
about your marriage, you could guarantee with nearly 100
percent assurance that your life together would significantly
improve—you'd at least want to know what it was.

Countless couples have discovered this "one thing" to be
the regular practice of *praying together*.

To someone who tends to devalue spiritual matters, this
may seem ridiculous. But the unity that grows between a man
and woman who regularly pray together forms an intense and
powerful connection. Within the sanctuary of your marriage,
shared prayer becomes a highly effective weapon in your battle
for marital longevity while also heightening your sense of
sexual intimacy. It can truly work wonders on every level of
your relationship.

When a husband and wife talk to God together, something
amazing happens. Jesus said, for example, "If two of you agree
on earth about anything that they may ask, it shall be done
for them. . . . For where two or three have gathered together
in My name, I am there in their midst" (Matthew 18:19–20).
Though Jesus' words apply to all believers, they certainly apply
to Christian marriages. United prayer actually ushers the
presence of God into your marriage in a special way, accom-
panied by the love, joy, and peace you long to experience in
your home. It happens each time you join hands together to
approach the throne of grace.

When you were joined as husband and wife, God gave you a wedding gift—a permanent prayer partner for life, someone who can help take all your praying to the next level. When you need wisdom on a certain decision, you and your mate can seek God together for the answer. When you're struggling with personal fears and insecurities, your prayer partner can hold your hand and intercede on your behalf. When you and your spouse are not getting along and can't seem to get past a particular argument or sticking point, you can call a time-out, drop your weaponry, and go with your partner into emergency intercession. Prayer should become your first response and your automatic reflex when you don't know what else to do.

It's hard to stay angry for long with someone you're praying for. It's hard not to back down when you're hearing your mate humbly cry out to God for mercy in the midst of your heated crisis. In prayer, a husband and wife remember that God has made them one. And in the grip of His uniting presence, disharmony blends into beauty.

The word Jesus used, in fact, about "agreeing" in prayer carries this idea of a harmonious symphony. When two different notes are played together, they create a fuller, more complete sound than either of them can accomplish on their own. Likewise, when we bring our divergent views and personalities together in prayer, God joins these together in harmony. Agreeing in prayer—even in the midst of disagreeing—pulls us both back toward our real center. It places us on common ground, face-to-face before the Father.

The church (which in Scripture has a marriage connotation with Christ) is a place where disharmony can sometimes flare up and derail members from their mission while disrupting their worship and unity. At times, when godly church leaders sense this taking place, they will break off further discussions and call the people of God to prayer. Instead of continuing the discord and allowing more feelings to be hurt, they will seek to restore unity by turning their hearts back to God and appealing together for help.

The same thing happens in our homes when we let prayer intervene at high points of disagreement. It stops the bleeding. It quiets the loud voices. It pauses our painful passion as we realize Whose presence we're in.

But prayer can do a lot more than just break up fights. Prayer is a privilege to be enjoyed on a consistent, daily basis. Praying for your spouse leads your heart to care more deeply about them. Hearing him or her pray for your needs, your protection, and God's blessings over your life is an intimate experience that can deepen your love and feelings for one another.

When you know that prayer time awaits you before going to bed at night, it will change the way you spend your evening. Even if your prayers are short and to the point, they'll become a standing appointment you each orbit your day around, keeping God in the middle of everything. Where He should be.

It's true that beginning a habit like this can initially feel foreign or awkward. But anything this powerful will surprise you with its long-term results as you actually try doing it. The more you practice it, in fact, the more it will become a natural part of your time together. And more importantly, God will be pleased when He sees you both humbling yourselves and seeking His face ... *together*.

You'll look back at this common thread that ran through everything from average Mondays to major decisions, and be so thankful you invested yourselves in this "one thing" that so deeply changes everything. This is one area where it's imperative that you agree to agree.

TODAY'S DARE

ASK YOUR SPOUSE IF YOU CAN BEGIN
PRAYING TOGETHER. TALK ABOUT THE BEST
TIME TO DO THIS, WHETHER IT'S IN THE
MORNING, YOUR LUNCH HOUR, OR BEFORE
BEDTIME. USE THIS TIME TO COMMIT YOUR
CONCERNS, DISAGREEMENTS, AND NEEDS
BEFORE THE LORD. DON'T FORGET TO THANK
HIM FOR HIS PROVISION AND BLESSING.
EVEN IF YOUR SPOUSE REFUSES TO DO THIS,
RESOLVE TO SPEND THIS DAILY TIME
IN PRAYER YOURSELF.

___ Check here when you've completed today's dare.

How did your mate respond to your request to pray
together? If you agreed to do it, what was it like? What did you
learn from it?

For a simple guide on how to pray together, see the Appendix, page 208.

In the morning my prayer comes before You. (Psalm 88:13)

DAY 38
Love fulfills dreams

Delight yourself in the Lord; and He will give you
the desires of your heart. —Psalm 37:4

What is something your spouse would really, really love?
And how often do you ask yourself that question?

Common sense tells us we can't give our wife or husband
everything they might like. Our budgets and account balances
tell us we probably couldn't afford it anyway. And even if we
could, we're too busy and probably don't have time.

But perhaps you've let your "no" become too quick of a
response. Perhaps you've become too reasoned and rational,
too automatic. What if instead of dismissing this thought, you
awakened your best to honor it? What might happen if the one
thing your husband or wife said you'd never be able to do for
them became the next thing you did?

Love sometimes needs to be extravagant. To go all out. To
set aside the technicalities, open up the floodgates of generos-
ity, and bless someone out of sheer delight. Is that thinking
too much like a teenager? Is that kind of love no longer on the
menu after this many years of marriage? After all, with the way
your relationship might be at the moment, wouldn't it be disin-
genuous to indulge your spouse if your heart's not in it?

Well, how about *putting* your heart in it. How about adopt-
ing a new level of love that actually *wants* to fulfill every dream
and desire you possibly can.

Did you know God loves with extravagance? He goes over
and above. He pours out freely beyond measure. The Bible says
He "lavished" His grace on us (Ephesians 1:8) and that Jesus'

love provides us with an abundant life overflowing beyond limitations (John 10:10). And we as His disciples are called to give that same kind of extravagant love—to give more than we're asked, to go the extra mile, to greatly exceed what is expected (Matthew 5:39–45).

Hasn't God's love met needs in your heart that way? You were living under a load of sin and regret. You thought you'd never earn your way back into His good graces. Yet He looked at you with love and said you didn't have to. He wanted you back and showed you mercy. As you turned to Him, He forgave you. "God, being rich in mercy, because of His great love with which He loved us, even when we were dead in our transgressions, made us alive together with Christ" (Ephesians 2:4–5).

So it wasn't when you were behaving like an angel that God chose to pour out His love on you. It wasn't because you were so deserving that He offered you His grace. Although you weren't a likely candidate, He loved you anyway. He freely paid the price for you. And He is the One your love is designed to imitate. His Word says that He loves cheerful, hilarious givers like Himself (2 Corinthians 9:7)—those who are willing to give in abundance out of pure delight.

What unexpected gift could you start saving up for that would overwhelm your spouse with love? A new dishwasher? Diamond earrings? A better car?

Where could you quietly arrange to get away for a romantic weekend, just the two of you? A friend's cabin? A nearby hotel? A cruise ship?

Not everything your spouse wants has a hefty price tag or can even be bought with money. You could secretly tackle a big project that has been on your mate's wish list for months.

Or really, your wife may just want your time and attention at home. She may want to be treated like a lady and know that her husband considers her a cherished treasure. She may want a warm embrace and to see in your eyes a love that chooses her all over again and will be there no matter what.

Your husband? The main thing he may want is just some greater respect. He may want you to acknowledge him as the head of the house in front of the children. He may want you to surprise him with a long kiss, or a love note, or to invite him home for lunch—with *you* as the dessert—when there's not even a birthday or anniversary to justify it. He may need to know that you still think he's strong and handsome to you.

Dreams and desires come in all shapes and sizes. But love thinks lavishly while taking careful notice of each one. So . . .

- Listen between the lines to discover what your mate is hoping for or really needing.
- Remember special things that are unique to your relationship, or see how you could create new memories during this season of your lives.
- Give when it would be a lot more convenient to wait.
- Daydream about opportunities so often that planning surprises becomes second nature.

We dare you to think in terms of overwhelming your spouse with love, to exceed all their expectations with your surprising kindness. Whether it's free or a financial sacrifice, it needs to reflect your thoughtfulness and a heart willing to express itself with extravagance. One of the greatest regrets people have later in life is that they didn't love others more fully when they had the chance. *Now is your chance.*

"What is something your spouse would really, really love?" It's time you started living out the answer to that question.

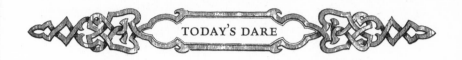

TODAY'S DARE

ASK YOURSELF WHAT YOUR MATE
WOULD WANT IF IT WAS OBTAINABLE.
COMMIT THIS TO PRAYER, AND START
MAPPING OUT A PLAN FOR MEETING SOME
(IF NOT ALL) OF THEIR DESIRES, TO
WHATEVER LEVEL YOU POSSIBLY CAN.

___ Check here when you've completed today's dare.

What has made you resistant to fulfilling your mate's desires in the past? How would it change your relationship if they knew their dreams were a priority to you? What desires are you attempting to meet?

God is able to make all grace abound to you. (2 Corinthians 9:8)

"I will fight to the very end for my marriage,
not because I have to, but because I want to."—Jay

DAY 39
Love endures

Love never fails. —*1 Corinthians 13:8*

When storms arise and conditions worsen, love chooses to endure through even the toughest issues. Though threatened, it keeps pursuing. Though challenged, it keeps moving forward. Though mistreated and rejected, it refuses to give up.

"Love never fails."

Many times when a marriage is in crisis, the spouse who is trying to make things work will go to the other, declaring in plain terms that no matter what has happened in the past, they are committed to this marriage. Their love can be counted on to last. They promise. But the other spouse, not wanting to hear it yet, holds their position. They still want out. They don't see this marriage lasting long-term. Nor do they even *want* it to last anymore.

The partner who has just laid his or her heart on the line, extending the olive branch, can't handle the rejection. So they withdraw their statement. "Fine. If that's the way you want it, that's the way it'll be."

But if love is really love, it doesn't waffle when it's not received the way you want. If love can be told to quit loving, then it's not really love. Love that is from God is unending, unstoppable. If the object of its affection doesn't choose to receive it, love keeps giving anyway.

Love never fails.

Never.

That's what Jesus' love is like. His disciples were nothing if not unpredictable. After their final Passover meal together, when Jesus told them they would all forsake Him before the night was over, Peter declared, "Even though all may fall away because of You, I will never fall away.... Even if I have to die with You, I will not deny You" (Matthew 26:33, 35). All the other disciples echoed the very same promise.

But later that night, Jesus' inner circle of followers—Peter, James, and John—would sleep through Christ's agony in the garden instead of supporting Him. Peter would later deny Him three times in the courtyard. Jesus' men had failed Him within hours of their sworn promises. Yet He never stopped loving them, and He came back to restore them . . . because He and His love are "the same yesterday and today and forever" (Hebrews 13:8).

When you have done everything within your power to obey God, your spouse may still forsake you and walk away— just as Jesus' followers did to Him. But if your marriage fails, if your spouse walks away, let it not be because you gave up or stopped loving them. *Love never fails.*

Paul endured beatings, intense persecution, and hardship throughout his life. He did it for one reason alone: because "Christ's love" compelled him (2 Corinthians 5:14). But how?

Of the nine "fruits of the Spirit" listed in Galatians 5, the first of all is *love.* And because the unchanging Holy Spirit is its source—the same Spirit who dwelled in Paul and in the heart of all believers—the love He creates in us is unchanging as well. No challenge or circumstance can put an expiration date on it. The love of God is anchored in the will of God, the calling of God, and the Word of God—all unchanging things. The Bible declares them "irrevocable" (Romans 11:29). "Heaven and earth will pass away, but My words will not pass away" (Luke 21:33).

The reason you were challenged a few days ago to build your marriage on the Word of God is because when all else fails, the truth of God will stand. Since each quality of love outlined in this book is based on the love of God, expressed in the unchanging Word of God, then your love, as a believer, bears the same, unchanging characteristics. It "bears all things, believes all things, hopes all things, and endures all things" (1 Corinthians 13:7). *Love never fails.*

When a marriage crumbles, couples often blame the failure of their relationship on "irreconcilable differences." But genuine love is a master at reconciliation. When love takes over, it compels us to humbly apologize and take full responsibility for our failures, then to fully forgive where our spouse has failed us. Over and over again. Resilient marriages are built on honesty, respect, commitment, forgiveness, and endurance. And love constantly inspires all of these things to grow and thrive within us.

So today, your dare is to put your unfailing love into the most powerful, personal words you can. This is your chance to declare in print that no matter what imperfections exist—both in you and in your spouse—your love is greater still. No matter what they've done or how often they've done it, you choose to love them anyway. Though you've been far from steady yourself in the way you've treated them and your marriage over the years, your days of being inconsistent in love are finished. You accept this one man or woman as God's special gift to you, and you promise to love them until death.

You're saying to your spouse, "Regardless of what has happened to us in the past, regardless of our many mistakes, and regardless of your feelings toward me—I choose to love you anyway. Now and forever."

Because love never fails.

TODAY'S DARE

SPEND TIME IN PERSONAL PRAYER, THEN
WRITE A LETTER OF COMMITMENT AND
RESOLVE TO YOUR SPOUSE. INCLUDE WHY YOU
ARE COMMITTING TO THIS MARRIAGE UNTIL
DEATH, AND THAT YOU HAVE PURPOSED TO
LOVE THEM NO MATTER WHAT. LEAVE IT IN A
PLACE THAT YOUR MATE WILL FIND IT.

___ Check here when you've completed today's dare.

What were some of the hesitations you had in writing this
letter? How do you expect your spouse to respond to it? How
did God help you in writing it, and what did the process teach
you about yourself?

_____

_____

_____

_____

_____

_____

_____

_____

He delights in unchanging love. (Micah 7:18)

"As we moved toward Day 40, we found ourselves asking for more. But now we know, as we move closer to God, He brings us closer to each other."—John

DAY 40
Love is a covenant

Where you go, I will go, and where you lodge, I will lodge. Your people shall be my people, and your God, my God. —Ruth 1:16

Congratulations. You've reached the end of the Love Dare—the book. But the experience and challenge of loving your mate is something that never comes to an end. It goes on for the rest of your life. This book may end at Day 40. But who says your dare has to stop?

As you view your marriage relationship from this point on, we challenge you to embrace it as a *covenant* instead of a *contract*. These two words sound similar in meaning and intent but are in reality much different. Seeing marriage as a contract is like saying to your spouse, "I take you for myself, and we'll see if this works out." But realizing it's a covenant changes it to say, "I give myself to you and commit to this marriage for life."

There are many other differences between covenants and contracts. A *contract* is usually a written agreement based on distrust, outlining the conditions and consequences if broken. A *covenant* is a verbal commitment based on trust, assuring someone that your promise is unconditional and good for life. It is spoken before God out of love for another.

A *contract* is self-serving and comes with limited liability. It establishes a time frame for certain deliverables to be met and accomplished. A *covenant* is for the benefit of others and comes with unlimited responsibility. It has no expiration date. It is "till death do us part." A *contract* can be broken with mutual consent. A *covenant* is intended to be unbreakable.

The Bible contains several major covenants as part of the unfolding story of God's people. God made a covenant with Noah, promising never to destroy all flesh with a worldwide flood (Genesis 9:12–17). He made a covenant with Abraham, promising that an entire nation of descendants would come from his family line (Genesis 17:1–8). He made a covenant with Moses, declaring that the people of Israel would be God's permanent possession (Exodus 19:3–6). He made a covenant with David, promising that a ruler would sit on his throne forever (2 Samuel 7:7–16). Ultimately, He made a "new covenant" by the blood of Christ, establishing an unending, unchanging legacy of forgiven sins and eternal life for those who believe in Him (Hebrews 9:15). Never once has God broken any of these covenants.

And then there's marriage—the strongest covenant on earth between two people, the pledge of a man and woman to establish a love that is unconditional and lasts a lifetime. In marriage, your wedding ring represents your covenant vows— not merely commitments you *hoped* to keep, but premeditated promises, spoken publicly before God and witnessed by others.

As you've read numerous times in these pages, keeping this covenant is not something you can do in your own strength. There's good reason why God was the One who initiated covenants with His people. He alone is able to fulfill the demands of His own promises. He alone is able to forgive the receivers of His covenant when they fail to uphold their part of the agreement. But the Spirit of God is within you by virtue of your faith in His Son and the grace He bestowed upon you in salvation. That means with His help, you now can exercise your role as a covenant keeper, no matter what may arise to challenge your faithfulness to it.

Especially if your spouse is not in a place of receiving your love right now, the act of covenant keeping can grow more daunting with each passing day. But marriage is not a contract full of escape clauses and exception wordings. Marriage is a covenant intended to avoid all avenues of retreat or withdrawal. There's nothing in all the world that should sever what God has joined together. Your love is based on a covenant.

Hundreds of years after the prophet Malachi recorded the following words, people are still wondering why God withholds His hand of blessing at times from some homes and some marriages. "You say, 'For what reason?' Because the Lord has been a witness between you and the wife of your youth, against whom you have dealt treacherously, though she is your companion and your wife by covenant. . . . For I hate divorce, says the Lord, the God of Israel, and him who covers his garment with wrong, says the Lord of hosts. So take heed to your spirit, that you do not deal treacherously" (Malachi 2:14, 16).

Every marriage is called to be an earthly picture of God's heavenly covenant with His Church. It is to reveal to the world the glory and beauty of God's unconditional love for us. Jesus said, "As the Father has loved me, so have I loved you. Now remain in my love" (John 15:9 NIV). Let His words inspire you to be a channel of God's love to your spouse.

The time is now, man or woman of God, to renew your covenant of love in all sincerity and surrender. Love is too holy a treasure to trade in for another, and too powerful a bond to be broken without dire consequences. Fasten your love afresh on this one the Lord has given you to cherish, prize, and honor.

Your life together is before you.

Choose to take hold of it and never let go.

We dare you.

TODAY'S DARE

WRITE OUT A RENEWAL OF YOUR
VOWS AND PLACE THEM IN YOUR HOME.
PERHAPS, IF APPROPRIATE, YOU COULD MAKE
ARRANGEMENTS TO FORMALLY RENEW YOUR
WEDDING VOWS BEFORE A MINISTER AND
WITH FAMILY PRESENT. MAKE IT A LIVING
TESTAMENT TO THE PRICELESS VALUE OF
MARRIAGE IN GOD'S EYES AND THE HIGH
HONOR OF BEING ONE WITH YOUR MATE.

___ Check here when you've completed today's dare.

What has God revealed to you during the Love Dare? How
have your views of your marriage changed? How committed
are you to God and to your spouse? Who can you share this
with as a testimony?

He has remembered His covenant forever. (Psalm 105:8)

"Our marriage will no longer be a marriage.
It will be a covenant with God."—Mary Beth

APPENDIX I
Leading Your Heart

WHAT IS THE HEART?

Your Identity. Your heart is the most important part of who you are. It is the center of your being, where the "real you" resides. "The heart of man reflects man" (Proverbs 27:19). As a person "thinks in his heart, so is he" (Proverbs 23:7 NKJV).

Your Center. Since your physical heart is in the center of your body and sends life-giving blood out to every living cell, the word *heart* has been used for centuries to describe the core starting place of all your thoughts, beliefs, values, motives, and convictions.

Your Headquarters. Your heart is the Pentagon of your operations. As a result, every area of your life is impacted by the direction of your heart.

WHAT'S WRONG WITH FOLLOWING MY HEART?

The heart is foolish. The world says "Follow your heart!" That's the philosophy of new age gurus, self-help seminars, and romantic pop songs. Because it sounds romantic and noble, it sells millions of records and books. But the problem is that following your heart usually means chasing after whatever feels right at the moment whether or not it actually *is* right. It means throwing caution and conscience to the wind and pursuing your latest whims and desires regardless of what good logic and counsel are saying. The Bible says, "He who trusts in his own heart is a fool, but he who walks wisely will be delivered" (Proverbs 28:26).

The heart is unreliable. People forget that feelings and emotions are shallow, fickle, and unreliable. They can fluctuate depending upon circumstances. In an effort to follow their hearts, people have abandoned their jobs to reignite a lousy rock band, lost their life savings following a whim on a horse race, or left their lifelong mate in order to chase an attractive coworker who's been married twice already. What seems perfect in the height of sweet emotion can feel like a stupid, sour mistake later on. This selfish philosophy is also the source of countless divorces. It leads many to excuse themselves from their lifelong commitments because they no longer "feel in love" or they think they must "find their soul mate."

The heart is corrupt. The truth is, our hearts are basically selfish and sinful. The Bible says, "The heart is more deceitful than all else and is desperately sick; who can understand it?" (Jeremiah 17:9). Jesus said, "Out of the heart come evil thoughts, murders, adulteries, fornications, thefts, false witness, slanders" (Matthew 15:19). Unless our hearts are genuinely changed by God, they will continue to choose wrong things.

Should I Ever Follow My Heart?

King Solomon said, "A wise man's heart directs him toward the right, but the foolish man's heart directs him toward the left" (Ecclesiastes 10:2). Just as your heart can direct you toward hatred, lust, and violence, it can also be driven by love, truth, and kindness. As you walk with God, He will put dreams in your heart that He wants to fulfill in your life. He will also put skills and abilities in your heart that He wants to develop for His glory (Exodus 35:30–35). He will give you the desire to be generous (2 Corinthians 9:7) and worship (Ephesians 5:19). As you put God first, He will step in and fulfill your deepest long-ings. The Bible says, "Delight yourself in the Lord; and He will give you the desires of your heart" (Psalm 37:4). But the only time you can feel good about following your heart is when you know your heart is submitted completely to God and intent on pleasing Him above all others.

Why Is Following My Heart Not Enough?

Because our hearts are so subject to change and so utterly untrustworthy, the Scriptures communicate a much stronger message than "follow your heart." The Bible instructs you to lead your heart. This means to take full responsibility for its condi-tion and direction. Realize that you do have control over where your heart is. You have been given the power by God to take your heart off one thing and to set it on something else. The following verses all communicate a message of leading your heart:

Proverbs 23:17	"Do not let your heart envy sinners."
Proverbs 23:19	"Direct your heart in the way."
Proverbs 23:26	"Give me your heart, my son, and let your eyes delight in my ways."
1 Kings 8:61	"Let your heart therefore be wholly devoted to the Lord our God."
John 14:27	"Do not let your heart be troubled, nor let it be fearful."
James 4:8	"Purify your hearts."
James 5:8	"Strengthen your hearts."

How Do I Lead My Heart?

First, you need to understand that your heart follows your investment. Whatever you pour your time, money, and energy into will draw your heart. This was true before you were married. You wrote letters, bought gifts, and spent time together as a couple, and your heart followed. When you stopped investing as much in the relationship and started pouring yourself into other things, your heart followed you there. If you are not in love with your spouse today, it may be because you stopped investing in your spouse yesterday.

Check your heart. One of the keys to successfully leading your heart is to constantly be aware of where it is. Do you know who or what has your heart right now? You can tell by looking at where your time has gone in the past month, where your money has gone, and what you keep thinking and talking about.

Guard your heart. When something unhealthy tempts your heart, it is your responsibility to guard it against temptation. The Bible says, "Above all else, guard your heart, for it is the wellspring of life" (Proverbs 4:23 NIV). Don't let your heart put money or your work above your spouse and family. Don't let your heart lust after the attractiveness of another man or woman (Proverbs 6:25). The Bible says, "If riches increase, do not set your heart on them" (Psalm 62:10 NKJV).

Set your heart. The apostle Paul taught, "Set your hearts on things above, where Christ is seated at the right hand of God" (Colossians 3:1 NIV). It's time to identify where your heart needs to be and then choose to set your heart on those things. You say, "But I don't really want to invest in my marriage. I'd rather be doing this or that." Exactly. You've set your heart on that in the past and you are stuck in a "follow your heart" mentality. But you don't have to let your feelings lead you any more.

Lust is when you set your heart on something that is wrong and forbidden. You can choose to take your heart off the wrong things and set it on what is right.

Invest your heart. Don't wait until you feel like doing the right thing. Don't wait until you feel in love with your spouse to invest in your relationship. Start pouring into your marriage and investing where your heart is supposed to be. Spend time with your spouse. Buy gifts. Write letters. Go on dates. The more you invest, the more your heart will value your relationship. This is what the Love Dare is all about—forty days of leading your heart back to loving your spouse.

Pray. Ask God to change your heart, to search your heart (Psalm 139:23–24), to test your heart (Psalm 26:2), to cleanse and create in you a clean heart (Psalm 51:10). Ask Him to open your heart to His truth (Acts 16:14) and to fill your heart with His love (Romans 5:5). He alone can change you from the inside out—from the hidden places in the core of your being—to help you with everything you say and do. God is the one Who can make the greatest impact on the condition of your heart!

May the Lord direct your hearts into the love of God and into the steadfastness of Christ. —2 Thessalonians 3:4–5

Appendix II
20 Questions for Your Spouse

Either on a date or during a private conversation, try using the questions below to learn more about the heart of your spouse. Allow the topics to raise additional questions that you may want to explore, but keep the mood and focus positive. Listen more than you talk.

Personal

1. What is your greatest hope or dream?
2. What do you enjoy the most about your life right now?
3. What do you enjoy the least about your life right now?
4. What would your dream job be if you could do anything and get paid for it?
5. What are some things you've always wanted to do but haven't had the opportunity yet?
6. What three things would you like to do before the next year passes?
7. Who do you feel the most "safe" being with? Why?
8. If you could have lunch with anyone in the world, who would it be and why?
9. When was the last time you were filled with joy?
10. If you had to give away a million dollars, who would you give it to?

MARITAL

1. What are three things I do that you really like?
2. What are three things I do that drive you crazy?
3. What have I done in the past that made you feel loved?
4. What have I done that made you feel unappreciated?
5. What are three things that I can work on?
6. Of the following things, what would make you feel most loved?

    Having your body massaged and caressed for an hour?
    Sitting and talking for an hour about your favorite subject?
    Having help around the house for an afternoon?
    Receiving a very nice gift?
    Hearing encouragement about how appreciated you are?
7. What things in the past do you wish could be erased from ever happening?
8. What is the next major decision that you think God would want us to make as a couple?
9. What would you like your life to look like five years from now?
10. What words would you like to hear from me more often?

Offer encouragement and a listening ear. Refuse to allow this to become an argument or time for you to criticize. Let this be a time for your mate to express themselves.

Appendix III
How to Pray Together

Devote yourselves to prayer; stay alert in it with thanksgiving.
—Colossians 4:2

Praying together as a couple is a priceless privilege with endless benefits. But to many this is a new idea and could be a little intimidating at first. Many people relegate prayer to standard situations. Church. Meals. Bedtime. Waiting rooms. But we miss daily opportunities to embrace the privilege God has given us to bring every need and concern to Him in immediate prayer . . . together.

As husband and wife, prayer together should not only preclude your days and your decisions, but it should also be your instant refuge at the first hint of fear, doubt, or concern.

- Any crisis should call you to immediate prayer together rather than panic. When you hear of a national disaster, a family emergency, or a friend diagnosed with cancer, take each other by the hand and rush headlong together to the throne of grace.
- Even at the discovery of good news, a united prayer of thanks will honor God for His blessings and deflect any temptation to take credit for it.

Start now, even in situations that are not particularly dire and dangerous, and let prayer become your automatic response for both the big and small of life ahead. At first, you might not know what to say. Don't let that worry you. The key is to be humble and honest before God by simply admitting what you are going through and then officially asking for His help. Do not try to impress your spouse with sacred sounding words.

Also, take advantage of the Lord's model prayer, found in Matthew 6:9–13. It is not a mantra to be repeated but a guide to be followed. Jesus didn't say this is *what* to pray, but *how* to pray. It contains as many as six different types of petitions in the space of its few words. You and your spouse can use it for direction as you pour out your hearts to Him.

Your praying can take on many forms:

- Thank Him for the good things He's done for you that come to mind, and praise Him for how awesome He is.
- Repentantly confess any sins you have committed and seek His merciful forgiveness.
- Pray by asking God specifically for what you need.
- Tell Him that you receive His love for you while also verbally expressing your love back to Him.
- Cry out in desperation for wisdom, strength, and guidance in the great and small decisions that lie before you.
- Surrender to Him and ask Him to change your heart.
- Ask Him to make your marriage something amazing that pleases Him.

Most important, bring yourself to a place where you are willing to say, "May Your will be done." Then go into the day, alive with expectancy of seeing Him work mightily around you and lovingly through you for His glory!

The next few pages contain some important "locks" and "keys" of prayer—attitudes, lifestyles, and responses that, according to Scripture, will either obstruct your experience of prayer or open it wider than ever before.

The Locks and Keys of Effective Prayer

Devote yourselves to prayer; stay alert in it with thanksgiving.
—*Colossians 4:2*

THE LOCKS: TEN THINGS THAT BLOCK PRAYER

1. Praying without Knowing God through Jesus

John 14:6—Jesus said to him, "I am the way, and the truth, and the life; no one comes to the Father but through Me."

2. Praying from an Unrepentant Heart

Psalm 66:18–19 NIV—"If I had cherished sin in my heart, the Lord would not have listened; but God has surely listened and heard my voice in prayer."

3. Praying for Show

Matthew 6:5—"When you pray, you are not to be like the hypocrites; for they love to stand and pray in the synagogues and on the street corners so that they may be seen by men. Truly I say to you, they have their reward in full."

4. Praying Repetitive, Empty Words

Matthew 6:7–8—"And when you are praying, do not use meaningless repetition as the Gentiles do, for they suppose that they will be heard for their many words. So do not be like them; for your Father knows what you need before you ask Him."

5. Prayers Not Prayed

James 4:2—"You do not have because you do not ask."

6. Praying with a Lustful Heart

James 4:3—"You ask and do not receive, because you ask with wrong motives, so that you may spend it on your pleasures."

7. Praying while Mistreating Your Spouse

1 Peter 3:7—"You husbands in the same way, live with your wives in an understanding way . . . and show her honor as a fellow heir of the grace of life, so that your prayers will not be hindered."

8. Praying while Ignoring the Poor

Proverbs 21:13—"He who shuts his ear to the cry of the poor will also cry himself and not be answered."

9. Praying with Bitterness in Your Heart toward Someone

Mark 11:25–26—"Whenever you stand praying, forgive, if you have anything against anyone, so that your Father who is in heaven will also forgive you your transgressions. But if you do not forgive, neither will your Father who is in heaven forgive your transgressions."

10. Praying with a Faithless Heart

James 1:6–8—"But he must ask in faith without any doubting, for the one who doubts is like the surf of the sea, driven and tossed by the wind. For that man ought not to expect that he will receive anything from the Lord, being a double-minded man, unstable in all his ways."

THE KEYS: TEN THINGS THAT MAKE PRAYER EFFECTIVE

1. Praying by Asking, Seeking, and Knocking

Matthew 7:7–8, 11—"Ask, and it will be given to you; seek, and you will find; knock, and it will be opened to you. For everyone who asks receives, and he who seeks finds, and to him who knocks it will be opened. . . . If you then, being evil, know how to give good gifts to your children, how much more will your Father who is in heaven give what is good to those who ask Him!"

2. Praying in Faith

Mark 11:24—"Therefore I say to you, all things for which you pray and ask, believe that you have received them, and they will be granted you."

3. Praying in Secret

Matthew 6:6—"But you, when you pray, go into your inner room, close your door and pray to your Father who is in secret, and your Father who sees what is done in secret will reward you."

4. Praying according to God's Will

1 John 5:14—"This is the confidence we have before Him, that, if we ask anything according to His will, He hears us."

5. Praying in Jesus' Name

John 14:13–14—"Whatever you ask in My name, that will I do, so that the Father may be glorified in the Son. If you ask Me anything in My name, I will do it."

6. Praying in Agreement with Other Believers

Matthew 18:19–20—"Again I say to you, that if two of you agree on earth about anything that they may ask, it shall be done for them by My Father who is in heaven. For where two or three have gathered together in My name, I am there in their midst."

7. Praying while Fasting

Acts 14:23—"When they had appointed elders for them in every church, having prayed with fasting, they commended them to the Lord in whom they had believed."

8. Praying from an Obedient Life

1 John 3:21–22—"Beloved, if our heart does not condemn us, we have confidence before God; and whatever we ask we receive from Him, because we keep His commandments and do the things that are pleasing in His sight."

9. Praying while Abiding in Christ and His Word

John 15:7—"If you abide in Me, and My words abide in you, ask whatever you wish, and it will be done for you."

10. Praying while Delighting in the Lord

Psalm 37:4—"Delight yourself in the Lord; and He will give you the desires of your heart."

Summary of the Locks and Keys of Prayer

1. You must be in a right relationship with God.

2. You must be in a right relationship with other people.

3. Your heart must be right.

APPENDIX V
How to Pray for Your Wife

1. That she would love the Lord with all her heart, mind, soul, and strength. (Matthew 22:36–40)
2. Find her beauty and identity in Christ and reflect His character. (1 Peter 3:1–3; Proverbs 31:30)
3. Love the Word of God and allow it to bloom her into Christlikeness. (Ephesians 5:26)
4. Be gracious, speaking the truth in love and avoiding gossip. (Ephesians 4:15, 29; 1 Timothy 3:11)
5. Respect you and submit to your leadership as unto the Lord. (Ephesians 5:22–24; 1 Corinthians 14:45)
6. Be grateful and find her contentment in Christ, not in circumstances. (Philippians 4:10–13)
7. Be hospitable and diligently serve others with Christlike joy. (Philippians 2:3–4)
8. Bring her family good and not evil all the days of her life. (Proverbs 31:12; 1 Corinthians 7:34)
9. Invite godly, older women to mentor her and help her grow. (Titus 2:3–4)
10. Not believe lies that would devalue her roles as a wife and mother. (Titus 2:5)
11. Be loving, patient, hard to offend, and quick to forgive. (James 1:19; Ephesians 4:32)
12. Have her sexual needs met only by her husband, and to meet his. (1 Corinthians 7:1–5)
13. Be devoted to prayer and effectively intercede for others. (Colossians 4:2; Luke 2:37)
14. Guide her home and children in a diligent, Christlike way. (Proverbs 31:27)
15. Provide no reason for her character to be slandered or to lose confidence. (1 Timothy 5:14)

How to Pray for Your Husband

1. That he would love the Lord with all his heart, mind, soul, and strength. (Matthew 22:36–40)

2. Walk in integrity, keep his promises, and fulfill his commitments. (Psalm 15; 112:1–9)

3. Love you unconditionally and stay faithful to you. (Ephesians 5:25–33; 1 Corinthians 7:1–5)

4. Be patient, kind, hard to offend, and quick to forgive. (James 1:19; Ephesians 4:32)

5. Not get distracted or cower into passivity, but embrace responsibility. (Nehemiah 6:1–14)

6. Become a hard worker who faithfully provides for your family and children. (Proverbs 6:6–11; 1 Timothy 5:8)

7. Be surrounded with wise friends and avoid foolish friends. (Proverbs 13:20; 1 Corinthians 15:33)

8. Use good judgment, pursue justice, love mercy, and walk humbly with God. (Micah 6:8)

9. Depend upon God's wisdom and strength rather than his own. (Proverbs 3:5–6; James 1:5; Philippians 2:13)

10. Make choices based upon the fear of God, not the fear of man. (Psalm 34; Proverbs 9:10; 29:25)

11. Become a strong spiritual leader with courage, wisdom, and conviction. (Joshua 1:1–10; 24:15)

12. Break free from any bondage, bad habit, or addiction that is holding him back. (John 8:31, 36; Romans 6:1–19)

13. Find his identity and satisfaction in God rather than temporary things. (Psalm 37:4; 1 John 2:15–17)

14. Read the Word of God and allow it to guide his decisions. (Psalm 119:105; Matthew 7:24–27)

15. Be found faithful to God and leave a strong legacy for future generations. (2 Timothy 4:6–8; John 17:4)

Appendix VI
How Can I Find Peace with God?

Even after going through Day 20 of the Love Dare, you may still be unsure about your relationship with God. But nothing should prevent you from receiving and experiencing His love for you at this very moment, and being able to love your spouse from this boundless reservoir of strength.

Here's how the Bible describes this supernatural reality:

God created us to please and honor Him. But because of our pride and selfishness, every one of us has fallen short of our purpose and dishonored God at different times in our lives. We have all sinned against Him, failing to bring Him the honor and glory He deserves from each of us (Romans 3:23).

If you claim to be a good person, be honest with yourself and ask if you have ever dishonored God by lying, cheating, lusting, stealing, rebelling against authorities, or hating others. Not only do these sins cause consequences in this life, but they disqualify us from being right before God and living with Him in heaven for eternity. Because God is holy, He must reject all that is sinful (Matthew 13:41–43). And because He is perfect, He cannot allow us to sin against Him and go unpunished, or He would not be a just judge (Romans 2:5–8). The Bible says that our sins separate us from God and that the "wages of sin is death" (Romans 6:23). This death is not only physical, but the resulting spiritual death brings separation from God for eternity.

What most people don't realize is that our occasional good deeds do not take away our sins or somehow cleanse us in God's eyes. If they could, then we could earn our way into heaven and negate the justice of God against sin. This is not only impossible, but it denies God the honor He deserves.

The good news is that God is not only just, but He is also loving and merciful. He has provided a better way for us to have forgiveness and come to know Him.

Out of His love and kindness for us, the Bible says He sent His only Son, Jesus Christ, to die in our place and shed His blood to pay the price for our sins. This provided a pure sacrifice and a just payment to God for our sins and allowed Jesus to receive the judgment we are due. Jesus' death satisfied the justice of God while also providing a perfect demonstration of the mercy and love of God. Three days after Jesus' death, God raised Him to life as our living Redeemer to prove that He is the Son of God (Romans 1:4).

God demonstrates His own love for us, in that while we were yet sinners, Christ died for us. (Romans 5:8)

For God so loved the world, that He gave His only begotten Son, that whoever believes in Him should not perish, but have eternal life. (John 3:16)

Because of the death and resurrection of Jesus Christ, we have been given the opportunity of being forgiven and then finding peace with God. It may not seem right that salvation is a free gift. But the Scriptures teach that God wanted to reveal how rich His grace and kindness are toward us by offering us salvation for free (Ephesians 2:1–7). He is now commanding all people everywhere to repent and turn away from their sinful ways and humbly trust Jesus for their salvation. By surrendering your life to His lordship and control, you can have forgiveness and freely receive everlasting life.

The wages of sin is death, but the free gift of God is eternal life in
Christ Jesus our Lord. (Romans 6:23)

If you confess with your mouth Jesus as Lord, and believe in your heart
that God raised Him from the dead, you will be saved. (Romans 10:9)

Millions of people around the world have found peace
with God through surrendering their lives to Jesus Christ. But
each of us must choose for ourselves.

Is there anything stopping you from surrendering your life
to Jesus right now? If you understand your need to be forgiven
and are ready to begin a relationship with God, we encourage
you to pray now and trust your life to Jesus Christ. Be honest
with God about your mistakes and your need for His forgiveness. Resolve to turn away from your sin and to place your trust
in Him and in what He did on the cross. Then open your heart
and invite Him into your life to fill you, change your heart, and
take control. If you are not sure how to communicate this to
Him, then use this prayer as a guide.

Lord Jesus, I know that I have sinned against You and deserve
the judgment of God. I believe that You died on the cross to pay for my
sins. I choose now to turn away from my sins and ask for Your forgive-
ness. Jesus, I'm making You the Lord and Boss of my life. Change me
and help me now to live the rest of my life for You. Thank You for giv-
ing me a home in heaven with You when I die. Amen.

If you just prayed sincerely and gave your life to Jesus
Christ, then we congratulate you and encourage you to tell others about your decision. If you really meant it, then you need to
take some important first steps in your spiritual journey.

First, it is essential that you find a Bible-teaching church and tell them that you want to obey Christ's command to be baptized. This is a great mile marker that allows you to publicly identify with Jesus, share your faith with others, and launch your new spiritual walk. Plug into your new church and start attending on a regular basis and sharing life with other believers in Jesus Christ. They will encourage you, pray for you, and help you to grow. We all need fellowship and accountability.

Also, find a Bible you can understand and begin to read it for a few minutes every day. Start in the book of John and work your way through the New Testament. As you read, ask God to teach you how to love Him and walk with Him. Begin to talk with God in prayer to thank Him for your new life, confess your sins when you fail, and to ask for what you need. As you walk with the Lord, take advantage of opportunities God gives you to share your faith with others. The Bible says, "In your hearts revere Christ as Lord. Always be prepared to give an answer to everyone who asks you to give the reason for the hope that you have" (1 Peter 3:15). There is no greater joy than to know God and to make Him known! God bless you!

APPENDIX VII
Overcoming Pornography

No temptation has overtaken you but such as is common to man; and God is faithful, who will not allow you to be tempted beyond what you are able, but with the temptation will provide the way of escape also, so that you will be able to endure it. —1 Corinthians 10:13

Pornography is idolatry. It creates an addiction of lust that leads a man or woman to surrender his or her mind, body, money, time, and purity in service to it. It becomes a god and perverted master.

When God created sex for a man and his wife alone to enjoy, He permanently linked its pleasure to marriage, love, intimacy, and lifelong commitment. Each of these keeps the sexual relationship meaningful and reinforces a couple's union in marriage. In holy matrimony, sexual pleasure is grounded in love, freely shared, and maintains its priceless meaning and many healthy benefits. There is no cost. No shame. No guilt. No regrets.

Pornography is the opposite. It strips sexual fulfillment of all its purposes. It disconnects sexual arousal from its foundation of love, marriage, and lifelong commitment, and reattaches it to lust, vanity, irresponsibility, and the perverted thrills of sin and shock imagery. Instead of sexual enjoyment being a reward from God, it becomes an undeserved, unearned, unholy, illegitimate pleasure with no purpose. It is like sexual cocaine that lures someone into a trap and then rapes his mind and conscience, leaving him addicted, numb, and demoralized. He begins caring less about the people he loves. He quits rejoicing over good things and grieving over sin. He feels guilty, dark, and dirty, spiritually distant from God and emotionally disconnected from his spouse. Not only that, he also gives Satan a foothold and permission to torment him now with condemnation, lies, and accusations. He's much worse off than when he started.

All addictions create a momentary spike in adrenaline that temporarily feels good but then leaves behind an even deeper void that causes more dissatisfaction than was there before. Because of this, pornography begs you to pursue its short-term thrill again, repeatedly lying to you that its "high" can pull you out of this pit. Lust just keeps breeding more lust. Then you get caught in a cycle that spirals downward and never seems to end.

If you ever feel a ravenous hunger for pornography, realize this: it is the last thing you need, and it will never satisfy you. Run. It is trying to use cheap lust to quench your thirst for genuine love. Satan always tempts you to meet legitimate needs in illegitimate ways. What you are actually hungering for is intimacy with God Himself, the only One who can fill the emptiness in your heart. Any lust in us reveals that we have not been feasting on the love from our heavenly Father (1 John 2:15–17).

Countless men and women have defeated pornographic addictions by learning to walk intimately and obediently with Christ in His Word and in prayer each day. Jesus told the woman at the well, "Everyone who drinks this water will be thirsty again, but whoever drinks the water I give him will never thirst. Indeed, the water I give him will become in him a spring of water welling up to eternal life" (John 4:13–14 NIV). His Spirit can fill and satisfy you in countless ways that pornography never can. So be courageous enough to recognize pornography for what it is: moral sewage and a pit of lies.

- It *lies*, telling you that your sexual pleasure is of higher importance than everything else.

- It *steals*, robbing you of marital intimacy, honor, and pure enjoyment of the marriage bed.
- It *pollutes*, coarsening your mind, numbing your conscience, and darkening your thoughts.
- It *belittles*, turning people made in God's image into prostitutes, mere sex objects of your lust.
- It *enslaves*, making you feel like you are powerless to stop or control your impulses.

This should disgust us. Look up and study the following verses that tell what else lust does to you. It chokes out the Word in your heart (Mark 4:19); leads you to destroy yourself and degrade your mind (Romans 1:24); causes inner struggle and strained relationships (James 4:1); creates a state of ongoing frustration, anxiety, and dissatisfaction (James 4:2); blinds you to what is most important in life (1 John 2:16–17); and invites the judgment and punishment of God (1 Corinthians 10:1–6). With these truths and grave warnings in mind, you must resolve before God to walk in complete honesty and purity (1 John 1:7), in full repentance and victory. Scripture shows us how to walk in freedom through the following ways:

- Do not allow lust to rule you anymore. (Romans 6:12)
- Put it completely out of your life. (Ephesians 4:22)
- Set your mind instead on things above. (Colossians 3:1–5)
- Remember that you now belong to Christ. (Galatians 5:24)
- Remember that God's grace empowers you to say "No!" to lust's demands and deceptions. (Titus 2:12)
- Run away when it tries to draw you back in. (2 Timothy 2:22)

- Be like Jesus, willing to suffer rather than sin. (1 Peter 4:1–2)
- Trust the Holy Spirit to fill you, empower you, and help you resist faithfully. (Galatians 5:16–25)
- Escape by believing the promises of God that He will meet your needs and never leave you. (2 Peter 1:4)

God has provided all you need to be completely happy and successful in life (2 Peter 1:3–4). And His plan involves you living free from pornography. If you have been enslaved to it in the past, you know firsthand how low it takes you. God never wants you again to see anyone undressed other than your spouse. Admit this. Human willpower isn't enough. You need God's grace.

So if you are addicted to pornography, confess it to God and someone else in your life who can spiritually hold you accountable (James 5:16). Begin memorizing His Word (verses like 1 Corinthians 10:13; 2 Peter 1:3–4; 2 Timothy 2:22; Philippians 4:6–8; Titus 2:12) and using it to fight off temptation. Feast on God each day. He is your source of satisfaction (James 1:17). Get radical about removing things that cause you to stumble (Matthew 18:9). During times of battle, shift your focus to praying for others to distract you from lustful thoughts (Ephesians 6:17–18). Stay accountable to godly friends, and never stop pursuing victory in Christ!

APPENDIX VIII
Seven Steps to Better Sex

Your level of enjoyment during sex is much more about what is going on in your heart, mind, and spirit than in your body. Too often, we don't prepare ourselves emotionally, spiritually, and relationally for sex, then we wonder why the act itself is only marginally satisfying. Since the sexual relationship is founded upon the strength of your commitment, love, and intimacy, it is important to get these three key elements right before you are physically together. When a husband and his wife surrender to God completely, know and love each other fully, and then give themselves to one another wholly, their intimacy and lovemaking launches to a new level of enjoyment. And not only this, God is greatly glorified in the midst of it all.

Remember, the idea of intimacy means to be fully known and then fully loved. This requires you both to first be honest and vulnerable with one another, and then to fully accept and affirm your mutual love and commitment to one another. Here are seven steps to help you experience these God-ordained blessings in your marriage and also take your sex life to a much higher level. Each step will increase your intimacy as you go through these one-by-one.

1. *Remove guilt.* Anything weighing on your heart or your conscience needs to be resolved. So spend a few minutes in prayer together, getting completely right with God so that no guilt is corrupting or weighing down either one of you. Recommit yourselves to Him and to His lordship over your lives.

2. *Remove bitterness.* Unresolved anger pours cold water on romantic fire. So in addition to getting right with God, also get

completely right with one another, not allowing any bitterness to exist between you. This means spending some time asking, "Are you hurt or angry with me? Is there anything between us? Have I wronged you in any way and not made it right?" Both of you must sincerely apologize and completely forgive one another of anything wrong that has come between you (Ephesians 4:32). This is vital to bringing about true oneness and the coming union you both desire.

3. *Remove stress.* Stress and worry distract our minds and weigh down our hearts. Pray for one another and for all the things you have been worried or stressed about. Pray for God to intervene in your circumstances. Pray for the future of your marriage and for Him to protect, bless, and strengthen your spouse. God calms our minds through prayer, brings emotional peace, and interweaves our hearts together.

4. *Fill up with God's love.* As you're praying, thank God for His love for you, and ask Him to make you a channel of His love to one another. Pray also for God to fill you with His Holy Spirit, that He will pour out His love, joy, and peace into your hearts . . . and through you to one another (Romans 5:5; Galatians 5:22).

5. *Overflow with thanksgiving.* Ungratefulness and selfishness both greatly diminish your level of satisfaction, not only in sexual intimacy but in all aspects of your life. It steals the joy from any experience and makes you feel used and devalued rather than celebrated and built up (Proverbs 23:6–8). Thanksgiving is a way to focus your mind on the positives about your spouse and increase their priceless worth in your heart and mind. So spend some time thanking your spouse for anything he or she has recently done for you, then let your spouse do the same for you. Appreciate and honor the contributions you make to one another's lives.

6. *Pour out affirmation.* Next, verbally affirm your love and long-term commitment to one another. Encourage each other with the things you most admire and respect in one another, the qualities and uniquenesses that still attract you to this one special person in your life. Cherish each other with your words, and receive your mate's words of love and devotion for you. "Pleasant words are a honeycomb," the Bible says, "sweet to the soul and healing to the bones" (Proverbs 16:24).

7. *Have selfless sex.* Celebrate your oneness and God's gift of your spouse. As you delight in your mate and become physically intimate with one another, both of you should focus completely on satisfying the needs and desires of your spouse before yourselves. Let your love unite in a feast of selfless affection. As you do, worship the Lord with your union!

> "*I have come into my garden, my sister, my bride;*
> *I have gathered my myrrh along with my balsam.*
> *I have eaten my honeycomb and my honey;*
> *I have drunk my wine and my milk.*
> *Eat, friends; Drink and imbibe deeply, O lovers.*"
> (*Song of Solomon 5:1*)

APPENDIX IX
The Word of God in My Life

Let this proclamation help you to rightly approach the Word of God.

The Bible is the Word of God.

It is holy, inerrant, infallible, and completely authoritative. (*Proverbs 30:5–6; John 17:17; Psalm 119:89*)

It is profitable for teaching, reproving, correcting, and training me in righteousness. (*2 Timothy 3:16*)

It matures and equips me to be ready for every good work. (*2 Timothy 3:17*)

It is a lamp to my feet and a light to my path. (*Psalm 119:105*)

It makes me wiser than my enemies. (*Psalm 119:97–100*)

It brings me stability during the storms of my life. (*Matthew 7:24–27*)

If I believe its truth, I will be set free. (*John 8:32*)

If I hide it in my heart, I will be protected in times of temptation. (*Psalm 119:11*)

If I continue in it, I will become a true disciple. (*John 8:31*)

If I meditate on it, I will become successful. (*Joshua 1:8*)

If I keep it, I will be rewarded and my love perfected. (*Psalm 19:7–11; 1 John 2:5*)

It is the living, powerful, discerning Word of God. (*Hebrews 4:12*)

It is the Sword of the Spirit. (*Ephesians 6:17*)

It is sweeter than honey and more desirable than gold. (*Psalm 19:10*)

It is indestructible and forever settled in Heaven. (*2 Corinthians 13:7–8; Psalm 119:89*)

It is absolutely true with no mixture of error. (*John 17:17; Titus 1:2*)

It is absolutely true about God. (*Romans 3:4; 16:25, 27;
Colossians 1*)

It is absolutely true about man. (*Jeremiah 17:9; Psalm 8:4–6*)

It is absolutely true about sin. (*Romans 3:23*)

It is absolutely true about salvation. (*Acts 4:12; Romans 10:9*)

It is absolutely true about Heaven and Hell. (*Revelation 21:8; Psalm
119:89*)

Lord, open my eyes that I may see truth and my ears to hear truth.

Open my heart to receive it by faith.

Renew my mind to keep it in hope.

Surrender my will that I may live it with love.

Remind me that I am responsible when I hear it.

Help me desire to obey what You say through it.

Transform my life that I may know it.

Burden my heart that I may share it.

Speak now, Lord.

Give me a passion to know and follow Your will.

Nothing more. Nothing less. Nothing else.

Notes

NOTES

NOTES

NOTES

NOTES

NOTES

NOTES

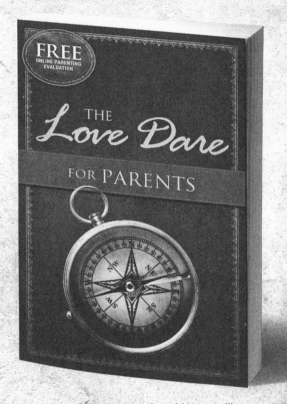

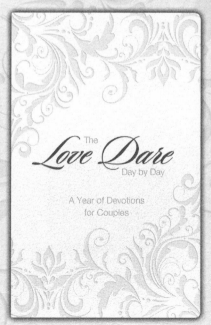

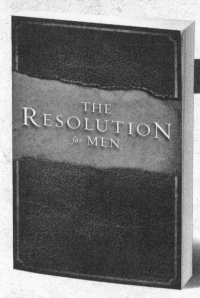

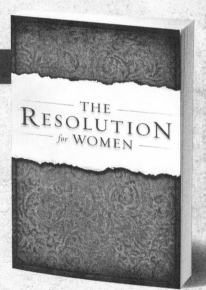